Saxophone Troubadour

Saxophone Troubadour
Musings on a Musical Journey

Al Regni

Saxophone Troubadour
Musings on a
Musical Journey

Copyright © 2022 by Albert G. Regni
All Rights Reserved

No part of this book may be used or reproduced in any form or by electronic or mechanical means, including information storage and retrieval systems, without permission in writing from the author.

Cover Design by Michael A. Sisti
Text Design by Michael A. Sisti
and Sara O. Sisti

Reviews of this book can be made on Amazon or Goodreads.com and would be appreciated.

Dedicated to
The beautiful women in my life,

Anna, Rosalie, Marissa, MaryAnn,
and of course, Sofie

Table of Contents

Prelude	1
Acclaim for Saxophone Troubadour	4
Prologue	7
Chapter 1	
Early Life and Growing Up 1936–1954	9
Chapter 2	
Off to College 1954–1958	27
Chapter 3	
You're in the Army Now 1958–1961	34
Chapter 4	
Moving to New York and Getting Started 1961	45
Chapter 5	
Broadway to Texas and Back 1963–2002	63
Chapter 6	
Recordings, TV, Movies, Studio Work, Teaching	98
Studio Work and Recording Dates	98
Movies	104
Teaching	105
Chapter 7	
Three Memorable Conductors	111
Leonard Bernstein	112
Leopold Stokowski	119
Pierre Boulez	125
Chapter 8	
A Few Tour Experiences 1968–2012	130
Chapter 9	
My Visit to North Korea, February 2008	148
Chapter 10	
Some Special Recollections	157
My Best Friend George	157
A Night at the Opera, 1987	164
Big Band Days of the 1960s, 1970s	167
Twin Peaks *Dance of the Dream Man*	172
David Gilbert and the Joking Monk	174

Nunzio *Toots* Mondello	175
New York Nightclubs	178
Golden Boy Memories	180
One Other Pleasant Recollection	180
Saxophone Quartets 1967–2014	182
ADDENDA: Al Regni Sax Quarter History	188
Chapter 11	
Partial Retirement from NY Music Scene	190
Conclusion	196
Acknowledgements	201
Al Regni Career Resumé	204
Special Thanks	216
Al Regni Through the Years (Photo Tribute)	217

Musings on a Musical Journey

♭Prelude

To say that Al Regni is the consummate musician with an illustrious career is an understatement by any measure. He's literally done it all, from big and small band jazz, orchestral and chamber work, arranging, teaching, Broadway shows, working for major entertainers of every flavor, and mentoring numerous musicians along the way, myself included. He has been so very generous in spirit, giving freely of himself at every turn, and a positive force to so many of us. Al has been a role model, good friend, mentor, and advocate for the majority of my career. I am forever grateful to this man, and all that he has done for the music, and the musicians. He has shown me how to carry myself as a professional musician, how to play a melody beautifully with poise, style and conviction, and how to be on the team in any number of ensemble situations.

Reading Al's memoirs was such a joy! It brought back so many incredible memories from the 40 plus years we have known each other. I felt nostalgic reading about the record dates, jingles, freelance orchestra gigs, sax quartet rehearsals, that made up a large part of my musical life along with the cast of characters that one would encounter day to day in NYC.

Al, along with George Marge, were instrumental in introducing me into the recording scene in New York. They

Saxophone Troubadour

both were so generous and helpful in this regard, and I am forever grateful. Al brought me into the New York Philharmonic circle as an extra when saxophone or doubling was called for, as well as doing the same with the American Ballet Theatre, Metropolitan Opera Orchestra, and others. I learned so much from these experiences. Al also generously introduced me to the Broadway pit orchestra scene, which was instrumental in providing much needed experience in the woodwind doubling world.

One of the highlights of my association with Al was being a member of the American Saxophone Quartet. The repertoire we played in that ensemble has had a lasting effect on my musicianship. I learned so much getting to play and blend with the incredible musicians in that group. Al was instrumental in showing me how the music should be interpreted, mainly through example. I am forever grateful to Al for instigating the commissioning of Rhythm of the Americas for sax quartet and orchestra which I composed in 2000. It was the thrill of a lifetime to have Leonard Slatkin lead the National Symphony Orchestra with the American Saxophone Quartet for 4 performances in 2001 at the Kennedy Center.

I recall a situation where Al asked me to sub for him on the remake of Brigadoon on Broadway back in the 80's. As was the custom, I went in and looked at the book during a performance. Al played so beautifully and made it all sound so very effortless. I mistakenly figured I could play this music with the same level of ease. Consequently, I did not spend nearly enough time preparing (taking the book home, recording the show, and really delving into the book in detail). Al's chair had 5 doubles, and once the show started notes were flying by fast and furious, with frequent instrument changes. I think I lost 5 pounds that day, and learned an important lesson concerning preparation in a

Musings on a Musical Journey

subbing situation. I thank you, Al, for giving me the opportunity to fall on my face and learn the hard way how things work.

I've gratefully been able to reconnect with Al, Marissa, and Rosie throughout the years on a regular basis. Blues Alley in Washington D.C. has been the meeting point for us, where the Yellowjackets regularly perform. It is always a joy to see everybody, and we inevitably tell stories of the years spent on the scene in NYC. You all have an incredible family!

Finally, I have to say it was so very enlightening to read Al's memoire. I learned many things about the man that I didn't know. All that I read completed the big picture of how Al became the amazing artist that he is, and how he sustained a 60-year career in music. I believe any aspiring musician would benefit greatly from reading Al's story. He is a power of example to us all in terms of what to do, what not to do, and how to be on the team. Thank you, Al, for sharing your history with us. And thank you, Al for your friendship and mentorship over the years.

With Love and Respect,
Bob Mintzer

Acclaim for Saxophone Troubadour

"The saxophone is only called for in a few works of the classical orchestral canon. Whenever I needed one, it was always Al who was first call. His versatility, virtuosity and innate musicality were always on display. And it didn't hurt that he has a great sense of humor. With so many years of experience, I am certain that his story will delight and entertain all readers."
Leonard Slatkin
Music Director Laureate
Detroit Symphony Orchestra

"Al Regni: *The Eagle;* Consummate artist, true mensch, lifelong friend and one of the two reasons I gave up the clarinet, describes his remarkable 60-plus year career as New York's Preeminent woodwind doubler."
Jonathan Tunick
Legendary Broadway Arranger/Composer

Musings on a Musical Journey

"When I moved to New York in 1980, hanging out at the various saxophone shops, the other saxophone players would speak of the New York luminaries. That is when I first heard about Al Regni. It would be decades before I met the man that I would hear when the NY Phil needed a saxophonist, but when I did, the man himself towered over the legend.

His career is wide and varied, as you will read about, so I won't go on about that. My time with Al has always been full of great stories and laughter.

Not too long ago, I was playing with the Orpheus Chamber Orchestra, and Al and his wife Rosy came to lend support. I spent a wonderful post-concert evening with them, swapping stories about life, love, and music. When I met with the guys and gals in the orchestra the next morning, the exuberance at the mention of being with him, and the equal level of disappointment at not seeing him themselves was not lost on me.

Al Regni is a saxophone legend; he's accomplished just about everything you can accomplish on the instrument. But his humanity tops it all. Immerse yourselves in the telling of his story. Enjoy the ride."

Branford Marsalis
Grammy Award Classical and
Jazz Saxophone Artist

"The ineffable Duke Ellington used to point out that there are only two kinds of music: 'good music and the other stuff', and I always saw my dear friend and admired colleague Al Regni as a living example of versatility and multitask-openminded musician. He has a great sense of humor too! I can't wait to read his autobiography."

Paquito D'Rivera
Multi Grammy award saxophone and clarinetist

"In the professional saxophonist's world Al Regni has done it all, and in this memoir, *Saxophone Troubadour,* he chronicles his legendary New York career as a top first-call instrumentalist. Along the way, in his easy conversational writing style, he gives the reader a glimpse into the secrets of his success. It's a must read for aspiring musicians, old pros or anyone who strives for excellence in any field."

Ramon Ricker
Professor Emeritus of Saxophone,
Eastman School of Music

Musings on a Musical Journey

Prologue

After a lifetime of playing music, I thought that many wonderful and some not-so-wonderful memories might be worth revisiting. It feels like such a short while ago that my pursuit of becoming a working musician began when in reality it's been over three-quarters of my life.

As I was starting out my New York City career in 1961, I was made aware that the changes that were going on during the mid-twentieth century were not ideal for a sustainable musical pursuit. I was constantly reminded by the players of the day that there was a possibility of the end of the live *music business,* as it was once referred to.

Much of what was predicted definitely came to pass with the termination of studio orchestras, live radio shows, and musical TV shows. Pop, classical, and commercial TV and radio advertising recording sessions were reduced in number, particularly through the 1990s. Club dates (i.e. weddings, industrial gatherings) utilizing live music became victims of the advent of disc jockeys.

It was a nebulous time for newcomers to the business. We were starting to feel like dinosaurs and were forced to reevaluate our commitments to the pursuit of our dreams. It was no different than what was happening in many other business fields. Becoming entrepreneurs in finding new ways of implementing our talents became a necessity.

Thankfully many new venues such as arts performance centers were springing up throughout the world. They provided some relief for touring possibilities such as jazz, rock, country, classical, and musical variety-type events. Broadway shows expanded as did their touring companies that would provide opportunities particularly for younger people who were willing to go on the road. Many music schools expanded their curricula to include jazz, pop, music business, production, film music, and media outlets. The explosion of video gaming has provided a lucrative field for an ever-expanding number of musicians.

Since my relationship with the music business covers the years roughly from 1950 through 2013, I certainly do not intend to dwell on the effects of what it was before or is to become after those years. As in any field, changes occur that seem to unfold more rapidly in the present day. I mention this because my effort is not to suggest that this is the way it will be, but simply to paint a picture of my own story. I believe the path that must be taken in any life adventure requires a strong dose of persistent dedication mixed in with reasonable thinking and a willingness to take chances.

The hope I have in telling my story is to encourage those with musical aspirations to follow their own dreams into an unknown, but exciting, future. Keeping one's open eyes along with a probing curiosity will oftentimes provide unexpected and rewarding opportunities.

Chapter 1
Early Life and Growing Up, 1936 – 1954

How do you define a life? Where do the influences suddenly make you the person you are destined to become? It all starts in childhood, of course, and is impacted by the family and friends around you. As I look back, I think of the people who influenced me and made me the person that I am. How did they do it? They each had their own methods; my parents, like many, were perhaps misguided but still driven by wanting to do the best for us. Their methods were vastly different: my dad used put-downs to motivate his children while Mom, in an attempt to compensate for Dad's rough manner, perhaps praised too much.

My sister Mary Ann was the darling of the family, always sunny and positive, despite her bout with polio at a very young age. She was, and is, super smart and excelled in school. Younger brother Freddie was mom's favorite and the main brunt of Dad's mockery. Dad's M.O. was to make Fred feel inferior to me, a method of intimidation that he also used to make everyone feel inferior to someone else. Later on in life, I would discover that same trait in some conductors, a way to control those under their authority.

Me? I was good at baseball and music, but not much else. Since professional baseball would obviously not be in my future, I pursued the only other avenue that I knew—

music. Being raised in upstate New York before, during and after World War II was an exciting time to be around music and musicians, even though I didn't realize it at the time.

During the first half of the Twentieth century the onslaught of European immigrants coming to the Triple Cities area of Binghamton, Johnson City and Endicott along New York's Southern Tier was enormous. Since this was a heavily industrialized area, jobs were plentiful and living there was to many of the new settlers, the start of the making of the American Dream. Because feeding one's family by being a musician was not an option to most of the newcomers, making a living had to be in other areas. Factory jobs were quite plentiful at the time and many of the musicians had to do their music making after hard daily work at the variety of factories in the area.

My father, who was first generation Italian, was born in upstate Binghamton, New York in 1912 shortly after his mother and father arrived in the U.S. from Italy. He was the first born of seven siblings, four brothers and three sisters. Named Americo in honor of his parents' immigration to the new country, but better known as Rico for most of his life, he was completely self-taught in everything that he did.

He was unable to complete high school because he needed to help the family make ends meet. He went to work as a machinist in the Endicott Johnson shoe factory where he met my mother in the early 1930s. While he was not formerly trained in the arts, he displayed promising talent and interest in drawing, woodworking and music. He exhibited extraordinary skills in all of his artistic endeavors, but because of economic and family requirements was not able to seriously pursue any one of them in depth.

Dad was a self-taught saxophone and clarinet player. In his younger years, he had a look that resembled Robert DeNiro with his slicked back black hair and sharp way of dressing in the latest, most fashionable suits; this earned him the nickname of Rico. To his credit musically, he seemed to instinctively understand how to fit in with any band, without getting in the way of other players.

Despite his somewhat difficult and critical nature, he seemed to respect the fact that I was a better player than he; at least, he made me feel that way. That fact didn't prevent him from letting me know when I could benefit from his business and musical experience. Although I sometimes resented this unsolicited advice, I now realize that he did help me to find my way in those early years.

Mother immigrated with my grandparents in 1920 from Reggio Calabria, Italy when she was seven. For similar reasons to my dad's, she left school while still in the fifth grade to assist her family both economically and to help raise her five brothers and one sister. Like my father she was a hard worker and was strongly determined to develop the skills necessary for survival in their new lives. She was also faced with the problems of learning a new language at an early age without the benefits of a formal education.

Both my parents, like so many immigrants, relocated with high hopes of attaining the American dream. I know my mother loved my dad even though he sometimes did not treat her in the best way. When she would get upset with him, which happened often, she would say to me, "If I had known my father was going to die so young, I never would have married your father."

But she would carry on her life as though nothing bad had happened.

My father, with his autocratic ways, was intent on making me into a song and dance kid. When I was about seven years old, he decided that I should take tap dancing lessons. This did not thrill me at all because I was a kid who wanted to do other things, but I knew that my objections did not matter. I tried to discourage him, as well as my dance teachers, by my lack of effort, but my father was firm and I deeply resented it.

My dance teachers were a pair of very nice, professional chaps named Sot and Ted, although I must admit that I never figured out who was Sot and who was Ted. They were probably frustrated Broadway dancers and I liked them both because of their patience and kind demeanor, so different from my dad. The first thing that hit me in the face when I arrived for my lessons was the acrid odor of nicotine emanating from both of them and every nook and cranny of the studio. At first, I wasn't sure what it was, but the kid in me found it to be exciting and even pleasant.

Everyone smoked in those days, and my desire to be one of those people probably started in that studio. I remember getting off on the smell and forgetting why I was there or what I was supposed to be doing. Was that the start of my life-long problems with a short attention span? The fact that they put up with my lack of enthusiasm and inability to remember the lessons was a testament to their dedicated teaching. After a couple of months of tortuous lessons, Sot and Ted decided that my lack of interest in the subject matter would keep me from progressing any further. Looking back, I feel somewhat guilty for being such a disappointment to two really good guys, but I suspect that they were glad to be rid of me. Strangely enough, I found myself missing them.

My relief at the end of the lessons was short lived, as my dad was then more determined than ever that I learn to be a song and dance man. Eventually, he got me to shuffle-step, shuffle-step, shuffle-step, step, and I was on my way, or so he thought to my quest of a vaudeville career. It was the early days of television, but most people still enjoyed theaters with live entertainment. We didn't know that those

Musings on a Musical Journey

days would soon be over. Live shows in movie theaters had been an important part of the entertainment landscape, but they were becoming rare. It was especially hard for Dad to accept that vaudeville was on the way out, as it had been such an important part of his life up to that point, and Dad didn't accept change willingly.

Almost every night, he hauled me off to our linoleum-floored basement to groom me into the next Fred Astaire. It never occurred to him that this was never going to happen. He would lose patience, scream and yell, and he even gave me a sharp whack every now and then. I missed the nice-guy team of Ted and Sot.

My father worked a five-day week in an environmentally compromised shoe factory with bad smells and back breaking work; his nerves were pretty shot before we even began. His methods of control were intimidation and fear. Eventually, he worked out a few routines, including a waltz clog, a soft shoe, a number which he called an eccentric dance, and our Big Hit—a two-man horse dance.

We performed our waltz clog, as the name suggests, in three-quarter time to the tune of *Casey Would Waltz with a Strawberry Blonde and the Band Played On*. This was one of the most popular tunes of the Vaudeville era. The dance was anything but a show stopper, but audiences seemed to be impressed with a father/son act, although we were no competition for Hines, Hines and Dad (remember Gregory, Maurice and Mr. Hines?)

Soft Shoe was my personal favorite; we wore straw hats and canes and sang and danced to the tune *Harrigan H-A-double R-I-g-a-n you see! Harrigan that's me!* I always felt embarrassed trying to impersonate an Irishman with our Italian brogues. In retrospect, I have fond memories of doing that routine—go figure! The eccentric dance was a bit weird. Our costumes were a cross between a hobo and a clown.

Saxophone Troubadour

Don't ask me what the point was, I just thought it was weird. The music we danced to was *Turkey in the Straw* and we didn't have to work too hard to act like a couple of rubes. With the wisdom of hindsight, I can now see that it was an audience favorite, even if a bit corny.

Our big number, however, was definitely the horse dance. Ever the artist and inventor, my dad rigged up quite an ingenious horse outfit using two large boxes for the body and a silly-looking face with ping pong eyes, large white teeth made of balsa wood, and an open smile that the audience found quite captivating. Secretly, my teenage embarrassment and angst made me only too happy to be covered up by the horse prop, with only my eyes slightly visible through a peephole in the horse's neck.

The arrival of my teens brought on a serious rebellion against these shows and dance routines, and I gained my dad's support to end them when I began to show serious interest in the clarinet and saxophone. Playing music was so much more exciting and satisfying to me, and dad was a big fan and supporter of those instruments.

I quickly found that practicing hard and becoming one of the better players in the school band at football games gave me a welcome edge with the ladies! The final step that got me out of the dance routines for good, however, was winning the audition for *The Ted Mack Original Amateur Hour* and Paul Whiteman's *TV Teen Club*. Dad, who was a frustrated musical star himself, wasn't going to stand in my way. After three stints on Ted Mack's show and one on the Whiteman show, I was, hallelujah, finally free of the dance act. In retrospect, it's likely that playing music was motivated by a way to free myself from dancing.

Aside from the music, my favorite extra-curricular activity in high school was playing on the varsity baseball team, the Johnson City High School Wildcats. Baseball was

Musings on a Musical Journey

and still is, my favorite sport and I had big dreams to someday play third base for the Brooklyn Dodgers. Around 1953, my dreams seemed a little closer to reality when our high school team won the New York State Southern Tier championship. We beat the champion Elmira High School team, for which the later-to-be-famous Ernie Davis* played for at the time.

Proud to say that I got the hit that started the rally to ultimately win the game, that would catapult us into the envious position of champs of our local division plus champions of the entire southern tier of New York State. This victory brought an invitation to a Brooklyn Dodgers tryout camp in upstate Greene, New York, where my dreams came to an abrupt halt. Two quick strike-outs and a less-than-ideal throwing arm led the Dodger scout to point me toward other forms of employment. It seemed at that time that a music career was the only remaining course of action.

Except for the early training as an attempt to make me another Fred Astaire, my childhood was pretty much as all boys had in the late 1930s to 1950s. Long days of playing outdoors, long walks to school with the added responsibility of corralling my brother and sister home at lunchtime to make some kind of meal for them while my parents worked in the shoe factory. Like all young boys, I tried to shirk work and responsibility to spend as much time as possible with friends.

*Ernie Davis was a star athlete even while in high school and the major league teams were offering him jobs before he even graduated. He was also sought after by pro football teams and after attending Syracuse University as an all-American running back and Heisman Trophy winner, he was immediately signed by the NFL's Cleveland Browns. His tragic death from leukemia at age 24 is one of the saddest days in sports history.

Saxophone Troubadour

We were young and unaware of possible dangers around us. I remember fondly our summer days at Bare Ass Beach.

We were just a bunch of too young, too reckless teenage boys, much like boys of the same ages (12 –15) in any decade, who didn't know the potential dangers of swimming in a river that was highly polluted and would later cause us some health problems. We just wanted to have fun and create some mischief.

The time was the late 1940s into the early 1950s and our group of school and neighborhood friends were bored and looking for adventure; so, we spent many of our summer days at the Bare Ass Beach, dubbed BAB, on the side of the Susquehanna River in Johnson City. We could see, feel, and even taste the pollution, but being young teens, didn't think that any of it would affect us. We were, after all, invincible and certainly tough enough to fight off some measly germs.

BAB was our favorite spot because it was protected from most people who lived nearby or happened to be passing by. There was a hidden cove where the railroad trestle crossed, so we felt confident enough to shed our clothes and swim au natural—hence, the nickname that we created for our spot.

There was a small area of muddy beach and nearby bushes that served as a convenient hanging place for our clothes. We not only ignored the human waste that flowed from sewage pumped and dumped from many area industries, including IBM, but we played with the balls of mercury from industrial waste that were often found floating in the river. I didn't learn until much later in life that the effect on me would be frequent nose bleeds that required cauterization. I would also learn at my fiftieth high school reunion, years later of course, that there had been

Musings on a Musical Journey

an unusual number of deaths of my classmates at relatively young ages. Cause: cancer.

But the young don't anticipate, and so we spent those carefree days climbing up the railroad tracks and maneuvering among the wood piers while the train rocked by, and even jumping to the river below, a distance of 15 to 20 feet. Some of the more daring boys would dive head first.

After much coaxing of each other, our favorite folly became striking many different poses and flashing the unsuspecting passengers on the passing Phoebe Snow train. We parodied Charles Atlas or Michelangelo's David; nothing pornographic. We knew the schedule of this train of the historic Erie Lackawanna Line; it was a classic passenger train, the kind no longer seen. It traveled between New York City and Buffalo, New York as it wound around the Delaware Water Gap, various New Jersey towns and finally into Penn Station in New York City.

The passenger view around that bend by our spot provided a great look at the fearless, or at least too macho to admit fear or hesitation boys whose aim was to shock these proper passengers of the day. We laughed heartily at the shocked faces that were glued to the windows of the train as it rumbled by. We were also too naïve, or at least wouldn't admit hesitation, to fear the poisonous snakes and the bullhead catfish with their sharp prongs that could cut your feet should you accidentally step on them.

We ignored the stench that emanated from the nearby rubber tire factory, and just took for granted the ever-present smog that hung over the area. That river was an important part of our young lives. We swam in it, caught fish to sell to the local rabbi for twenty-five cents, and smoked purloined cigarettes on our BAB. It was hardly a healthy upbringing, but I look back on it just the same and

Saxophone Troubadour

think of the clueless young boys who, even though perhaps in danger, thought they were in paradise.

Of course, swimming at the BAB was not the only thing that occupied the time and energy of the young troublemakers. Like so many kids in our youth, we usually played outdoors for most of the time when we weren't in school, and our parents didn't worry about us. We knew to be home when the family sat down to dinner. At about age 12, I had a burgeoning interest in all kinds of ball games, mostly baseball, but I liked football also and we boys often played pick-up football games on the open fields around our homes.

On one particular day, we had all gathered in the field for a competitive game. I remember these boys like it was yesterday. There was Jim McDonough, the guy we were all afraid of. Once he shot me with a bb gun because he didn't want me to leave his basement when I was trying to go home. He was just a nice guy who liked to act tough and show us that he was our leader and main mischief-maker.

Don Brewster was the handsome one in the group and he always seemed to get the girls. I guess I was a little jealous of him. George Hughes was cute, but small of stature. Foz was prone to epileptic seizures. In our ignorance of what to do when he started these, we would slap his face. The last of the gang was Bernie Sterner.

On that fateful day, we were playing a free-for-all game of football. This was a game where only four or five players were available, not enough for a true football game. The object was for one boy to throw the ball up into the air, while the others scrambled to catch it. The boy who got it would then run like hell to reach the goal line.

On this day, I dove to tackle the receiver, who sidestepped, which caused me to hit a clothesline pole behind him—hard. It broke my nose and smashed it to one

Musings on a Musical Journey

side of my face. I looked a lot like a Picasso painting. Later, the doctor fixed my nose by pulling it back into place and taping it. I wore that tape and sported a swollen nose for about six months. Predictably, the kids at school found my situation hilarious and one of them dubbed me *Eagle Beak* and it stuck!

In college, I told that story to a friend and was thereafter dubbed *Eagle*. Flash forward to 1963 and a gig at the Westchester County Dinner Theater. The leader of the band and piano player Howie Danzinger, together with the sax, clarinet and flute player Howie Rittner, liked to give nicknames to the band members. Because of the downward curve of my nose, they decided to call me *Eagle*.

All the other band members got their own nicknames. Jonathan Tunick's role was to write charts, so he earned the name *Tunesmith*. Howie Danzinger was *Potato* because of the wiry tufts of hair on his head. We also had a rabbit, a raccoon and a weasel. This two-year gig was one of the most fun of my career, and we still have a good laugh about it.

I went from being self-conscious about the kids calling me *Eagle Beak* to being proud of the title since I knew it was a sign of affection from the boys. The name was further solidified when a composer wrote a suite in the 1990s with a movement of an eagle titled *Flight of the Eagle* and then another used my moniker to write a composition called *Eagle Patrol*.

The two great local industries in those years were IBM which was founded in neighboring Endicott, New York and the Endicott Johnson Shoe Company which had factories in Binghamton, Johnson City and Endicott. Fortunately, the owners of both companies recognized the abundance of musical talent that was available as well as the need for added cultural benefits.

Saxophone Troubadour

Hence both companies formed bands and encouraged the artistic cultures that so many of the European settlers had been accustomed to in the *Old Country*. Concerts in the numerous park band gazebos as well as holiday and patriotic parades were regular features in the communities. Seeing my dad all decked out in his blue and silver Endicott Johnson band uniform were proud moments both for him and me.

Naturally a friendly rivalry developed between the two bands. The IBM band represented the blossoming hi-tech world and seemed to have the slick artistic edge but the European suaveness of the EJ Band had a charm that was unsurpassed. As a youngster I was particularly fortunate to have been exposed to some wonderful musicians who, even before I realized it, gave me concepts of musicianship that stayed with me throughout my life.

There were players on all instruments that brought European concepts and traditions in all types of music. The various ethnicities included Italian, Polish, Slavic, Germanic, and Irish as well as a variety of American pop styles that emerged at the time. Live music was in abundance before the overwhelming population became enamored with TV. Many night clubs and bars had live music groups representing all of the ethnicities.

As in so many of the human endeavors of the time, the European musicians featured melodic style as a representation of their individuality. Playing a note or a line with a beautiful tone quality that was rich with vibrato was the hallmark of the artist. In later years technical wizardry became king and anyone not able to play at break-neck speeds would be overlooked. The big bands of the 1930s through the 1950s featured melodic styles as represented by the likes of Benny Goodman, Tommy and Jimmy Dorsey, Artie Shaw and Glenn Miller, as well as scores of others.

Musings on a Musical Journey

Style was well represented in the way people dressed as well as the way they lived their lives.

Most musical associations in my teens (1946–1956) were a consequence of my Italian heritage. Being able to play in the Endicott Johnson Worker's Band, even though I was a student and not a worker gave me exposure to some excellent musical role models as I mentioned earlier. The solo clarinet player was Serge Clementi, a recent immigrant from Italy who impressed me not only as a fine clarinetist but also with his kind encouragement, especially to us younger players. Serge was not much over five feet tall but he carried himself with a dignified posture that gave him a much taller presence. He was constantly smiling and the purse of his lips when playing the clarinet sometimes exaggerated the formidable size of his distinctly Roman nose.

The solo cornetist, James Cordi, also of Italian descent, was the local answer to the famous English cornetist, Herbert L. Clarke. Mr. Cordi was easily the most celebrated member of the band. Whenever there was a prominent cornet passage his presence would be felt with the glowing sparkle of his tone quality. The wide European vibrato that he displayed exuded passion and style that was an extension of his suave radiant persona.

All wind bands that play military marches must have a strong tuba player, better known as a Sousaphone player. The EJ Band had a fine one in the person of Tony DiRitis. His steady rhythmic bass notes were extensions of his serious determined personality.

My personal favorite band member however, was the bass drummer Nicolae. So, how could a bass drummer be of any consequence? Nicolae was an education in musicianship. I loved to observe him preparing his precious instrument as if it was built by Stradivarius. The way he would fuss over the various cloth or leather materials that would dampen the instrument to just the right sound, was a lesson in craftsmanship.

Until I witnessed Nicolae in action, I never realized there was more to playing a bass drum than just hitting it and making it go boom. With his spectacles balancing precariously on the tip of his nose, Niclolae's slim body would crouch over the instrument with his finely tuned ear close to the rim to be aware of every nuance. He would encircle the big drum as if the instrument was an extension of his body. It had to emit just the right sound, coupled with the exact rhythm for that music and have a crispness that was undeniable yet full of flair and dynamic artistry.

The musical qualities he created remain embedded in my mind's ear to this day. I don't ever remember Nicolae without a stogie protruding from the corner of his mouth. I would go so far as to say it was a trademark of the studious yet humble image that he displayed. Although he was quite slim and a bit hunched over, his stature was that of a distinguished gentleman. He was a fine example of the dignity in being an artist. Even now I'm amazed that a bass drummer left me with such a strong impression of the noble pursuits of a serious music maker.

Although I never studied music personally with any of those people or knew them personally, I'm amazed after all of these years how much there was to be learned just by observing and listening to them. They were an education in so many ways that I was unaware of until many years later.

My first sax and clarinet teacher's name was Gino Calistri. Becoming his student at age 13 was a proud moment of my life. Mr. Calistri was the top saxophone and clarinet player in our area and a wonderful model of a musician. He was always encouraging and proud of any accomplishments his students achieved. Gino, as he was affectionately known, had a smile that could brighten a room. I remember his portly body adorned with the popular high waist suspendered pants reminiscent of the be-bop zoot suit. Gino's personality exuded warmth which also was a trademark of the beautiful sounds he made on both the clarinet and the saxophone. I remember him with much gratitude for the inspiration that he provided. Gino Calistri was an Italian mensch.

Gino was a close friend and colleague of local legendary trumpeter Dick Perry. Dick became a favorite of songwriter and Broadway composer Jule Styne. Mr. Styne wrote featured solo parts for Dick in several hit Broadway shows including *Gypsy* and *Funny Girl*. Mr. Perry was known as Broadway's premier trumpet player by the leading critics and musicians of the day. I was honored to work with Dick on several occasions during my years on Broadway and in the recording studios.

During my middle and late teens, I was fortunate to also have been a member of a Polish polka band. Andy Polakis was an accordionist and the leader of what was billed as Andy Polakis and The Silver Crown Orchestra. I was the third Sax/Clarinet player and sat between two fantastic technical wizards on both instruments. The agility and articulate way they conquered the mazes of notes associated with the Polish polka music was and still is embedded in my mind's ear. I am so grateful for their patience and urgings to a wet-behind-the-ears novice in grooming my abilities to match their skills. The first tenor sax player Irv Mrazek was in many ways a mentor and strong musical role model not only in his tremendous skills but in his high degree of professionalism.

For my career, these people were the treasures of my musical upbringing. The style and dignity they all brought to such a noble pursuit left an indelible mark that

Saxophone Troubadour

benefitted me in later years. I indeed have much to be grateful for in having highly talented wonderful human inspirations in my life.

The decision to pursue a career in music brought with it many significant issues. Most important to me was my insecurity about whether, despite my ability and inclination toward playing, that I could actually be successful as a professional instrumentalist. At the time, my concept of a player was to succeed in the world of commercial studio recording. In 1954, the radio, television and recording studios were booming and I longed to join the elite musicians who worked in live TV and musical venues. Although it was early days of television, many radio shows were dependent on live musicians to provide the backdrop for their dramas and musicals.

My experience on Ted Mack's Amateur Hour had given me a taste of what I longed to pursue in the Big Apple. Realizing what serious preparation and commitment this would take from me, I began to audition for music schools. By some miracle, I was accepted to the prestigious Eastman School of Music in Rochester, New York. This was a shock to both me and my father. At my audition, I was told that a requirement of my pursuit of a clarinet performance major was that I must develop an acceptable level of competence on the piano. At the time, this was a bit unnerving as I had no competence whatsoever in that area. I immediately embarked on the task of developing some piano chops.

My search for a teacher began at the Capitol Theater, a local movie house in the center of Binghamton, about five miles from my home. I knew, from the frequent visits that my dad and I made to the theater, that the pit band there was very good and that, as with many other theaters in those days, the band played twice a day between the featured films. This practice was a carry-over from vaudeville and was reflective of what was happening in venues like Radio City Music Hall, a place where I dreamed of performing one day.

Getting in touch with the pit band leader was not difficult, although I was apprehensive about approaching him with my request to study piano. I just assumed that I would be given the brush-off since he was a big deal and I a rank amateur. On the phone, I quickly explained that I wanted lessons but had no previous experience. To my surprise, he asked no questions, only assigned me a time to meet at his studio.

I was excited for the opportunity to learn from this professional, artistically competent man who so obviously kept tight control over the other members of the band. He always managed to show that he was the main attraction as he and his piano sat perched atop a raised podium in the middle of the orchestra. Aptly named Don Grey, he had a mane of silvery grey hair enhanced by his pristine white tie and tails. All of it seemed to reflect him as a giant in the ebony glow of the piano. I was in awe. In later years, I was struck by the similarity of his playing and style to that of the favorite of all conductors that I worked with—Leonard Bernstein.

I wasn't in the studio for more than ten minutes when his first words brought me back to earth with a loud thunk. Mr. Grey began my lesson by asking why I wanted to learn to play the piano. In my eager youthful enthusiasm and pride in my recent achievement, I replied, "I have just been accepted to the Eastman School of Music and I will start there this fall. Piano study is a required addendum to the instrumental major course."

To my shock and dismay, he quickly retorted, "Tell me why you want to go to music school."

Saxophone Troubadour

Forging ahead, I tried to explain that my acceptance was a great honor. I still hear his next comment in my head almost 65 years later. "Don't go to music school or even think of music as a profession or you'll end up being a bum."

This might have been the teacher's way of testing my resolve, but it was also the end of my tenure as a student of Mr. Grey. Instead, it was the start of a long journey to prove that I was capable and willing to do whatever it took to make a career in music. I never became an accomplished pianist, but that lesson gave me something much greater, the motivation to succeed. Over the years I have referred to it as the best advice I ever got, since it worked as reverse psychology, spiking a young man's drive.

Chapter 2
Off to College, 1954 – 1958

It was September 1954 that the beginning of the most impressionable part of my life was about to start. Mother, father, and I set out from our New York upstate hamlet of Johnson City for the scenic drive northwest to Rochester, New York, home of the Eastman School of Music.

Passing through Ithaca, New York, and proceeding northwest along the shores of wondrous Lake Cayuga to our final destination, we traveled a series of single-lane roads. This was before the initiation of the federal Interstate Highway System in 1956. It wasn't until many years later after experiencing extended world travel that I became fully cognizant of just how beautiful is this part of the world in which I was born and raised.

Other than a couple of trips to New York City, my travel experiences were quite limited at that time. As the feeling of any youngster leaving home for the first time, I experienced a mixture of apprehension and exhilaration.

In 1954 the Eastman School of Music was not equipped with student housing for male students. There was only one dormitory and that was exclusively for women. Therefore, the first task at hand was to scour the streets neighboring the school in search of a place to live. This was a challenge for someone who did not know his way around the map. I

Saxophone Troubadour

had one contact from my hometown, longtime pal Richard Woitach. After my unsuccessful attempts in finding any available rentals, I decided to look him up to see if he had any suggestions.

Winding through a maze of side streets in an older section of town I discovered Richard's location at 160 Scio Street. This was a collection of old Victorian-style homes that were formerly single-family residences, some of which had been taken over for student rentals. There was quite an assortment of tenants living at this address as I soon discovered after ringing the doorbell.

Answering the door was a spunky energetic chap who was welcoming and helpful. His name was John Veith and he quickly became one of my closest life-long friends. He noticed my desperation and offered a temporary spot to camp out in his room until I could find a place.

It turned out to be a permanent residence for the entire school year and carried over to the following year when we became roommates in the newly finished male dormitory. John was a close friend, good role model, and highly talented individual who went on to a very successful career. In later years he became the pianist and conductor for several name singers including Keely Smith.

The owner of the house was a ninety-five-year-old woman, Mrs. Vadas. Unfortunately, or possibly fortunately for us tenants, she was extremely hard of hearing and had very poor eyesight. She seemed oblivious to the happenings in her surroundings. She sometimes would lose her way around the house and end up in our room and we were happy her vision was not good, especially when women were visiting in the room. Her strict policy was that the residence was men only.

Living in this old structure were eleven rambunctious horny youths divided among two bedrooms on the first floor and three bedrooms on the second floor. All were good people but prone to lively parties and loud record players, not to mention that we were a mixture of instrumentalists. We had two pianists, a bassoonist, a tuba player, bassist, trumpeter, trombonist, cellist, violinist, a French hornist, and me (clarinet) all of whom, became successful in their careers.

In many ways living in that house during that time was an education in itself, even though it was not conducive to attaining good grades at school.

Required school subjects such as English, Psychology, and Fine Arts were not my cups of tea during my ignoramus freshman year. My only interest was playing sax and clarinet. And, owing to my lack of maturity, I saw no value in anything other than playing music. An example of this was in an early English class. The assignment was to write an essay on one's instrument of choice. My early giveaway was titling the essay SAXAPHONE. The first correction (of which there were many) made by the instructor was the importance of learning how to spell SAXOPHONE. How I ever got through high school I will never know.

The total lack of discipline resulted in poor grades at the end of the first semester. My clarinet teacher Bill Osseck revealed that the school had notified him of my poor showing. And unless I got my act together, I would no longer be fit to continue at this prestigious institution as a performance major. That was all I needed to get down to work and things got better in the second semester. It was also a blessing in disguise in that I changed majors to music education, providing a teaching certificate which proved important in the years that followed.

In that first semester, it also did not help that my youthful sex drive was a constant source of preoccupation. I hadn't been at college very long when I fell hard for cute

Saxophone Troubadour

Janie. It was pure puppy love and when she decided to dump me my heart was broken. It took me a while to get over that and to pay full attention to my musical pursuits.

In my second year I had a brief relationship with the gorgeous Kay Johnson which unfortunately had bad timing. She was as beautiful on the inside as she was on the outside. I did manage to see her while in Hawaii in 1981. But by then she was married and settled into a comfortable life in Honolulu. I had recently been formally divorced, so once again timing was not in the books.

Being a saxophonist allowed me to become a member of the prestigious Eastman Wind Ensemble founded and led by the legendary Frederick Fennell. Becoming a member of this group was an honor, especially since it happened during my freshman year. I was part of this group for all of my four years at the school.

The ensemble not only gave first-class concerts but made a series of recordings during those years that have become classics and remain shining examples of wind band music to this day. Dr. Fennell was also a huge influence on my musical upbringing. I am eternally grateful for having had the opportunity to have worked under his inspired conducting.

The teachers at Eastman were exemplary mentors as both educators and performing artists. Flutist Joseph Mariano, clarinetist Stanley Hasty, French hornist Morris Secon, Trombonist Emory Remington, and my teacher William Osseck are just a few of the names that I will always be indebted to for building a personal foundation and sending me out into the real world on a good path.

I cannot praise my student colleagues enough learning and growing together with such incredible talents. It was of major importance to my musical career. The saxophone sound that I carry in my mind's ear was and still is, that of

Musings on a Musical Journey

Jack Carey. Jack did not follow up with a music career which I consider unfortunate, but I am sure he had good reasons. The warmth and depth of his tone quality were unparalleled in my opinion. In addition to the saxophone sounds made by Charlie Parker and Jimmy Abato, Jack was just as much a personal tonal inspiration. I never got to know Jack very well, but the quality of his saxophone tone quality remains with me.

My dear and lifelong friend Syd Hodkinson was an inspiration not only for his great musicianship and dedication but for his great support throughout the years. George Marge was another strong influence, as I relate with more detail in chapter four. These were two of my lifelong buddies and major forces. John Veith, who I, unfortunately, lost touch with, still warms my soul with the friendship and caring we had for each other. Several others were not necessarily close friends but had a bearing on the direction I took in later years.

Extracurricular activities were important steps in bringing critical musical experiences to enhance the basic educational tools. All these proved valuable in all facets of my future years.

When my buddy George Marge graduated two years before me, he recommended that I fill his spot with a well-known local society band. The band leader was a drummer and prominent Rochester, New York personality named Carl Dengler. Mr. Dengler was a blind man and as a result, had amazing hearing. I was impressed with his complete awareness of every player in the eight-piece ensemble. As a wet behind the ears cocky jazzer, I had much to learn from his well-grounded musicality.

I was indeed fortunate that he recognized my ability and was patient with my inexperience as he passed along many valuable insights into basic music-making as well as

Saxophone Troubadour

business practices. Working in this ensemble was a school away from school and it was an important part of my life for nearly two years.

During my last year at the Eastman School, I was hired to play in a Rochester nightclub six nights a week. It was a valuable learning experience in more ways than one. First, foremost and somewhat notoriously, it was a strip club but also featured a singer and/or a dance act as well as a stand-up comedian. The four-piece combo consisted of piano, acoustic bass, drums, and me on sax.

The leader of the group was pianist John Butler and he was as much a teaching professor as anyone I had in music school. He was insistent that I become knowledgeable of most of the Great American songbook and learn the tunes properly with the right notes and the right style. He was the consummate professional and I was fortunate to have been playing with him and under his astute patient guidance, especially during those formative years.

Performing at that venue consisted of playing the opening act which usually had written arrangements, followed by an intro for the comic and then the featured stripper whose act was climaxed by the raunchy rendition of the infamous tune *Night Train*. Before, between, and after the show we would play jazz-like tunes mainly for background sounds. All-in-all it was a good job from a musical standpoint even though it was not Carnegie Hall. But, just as important, it helped to fund a large portion of my college tuition.

A major event in my life occurred in my third year of college when I began dating and eventually married Charlotte Westcott. Even though the marriage was not ultimately successful, it was the start of 24 years together that produced the miracle of our daughter Marissa and eventually resumed as a friendship.

Musings on a Musical Journey

Somehow, I managed to finish four years at one of the world's greatest conservatories and land on my feet. It further resulted in my being awarded a distinguished alumni award in 2019, an honor I deeply treasure. I am eternally grateful for having had the good fortune of being a graduate of the Eastman School of Music and for the foundation it provided for a career in such a noble profession.

Without the wonderful guidance and influences of the professors and talented student colleagues that I was fortunate to have learned from, I doubt that my good fortunes would have been possible. Every one of the people mentioned in this chapter had a profound impact on my career during those critically important formative years.

Chapter 3
You're in the Army Now, 1958 – 1961

1958 was a pivotal year for me, as I was getting ready to graduate from the Eastman School of Music in April and wondering where life would take me. Like all young people, getting ready to face the *real world* was a challenging task that was a bit daunting. The safety and carefree days of college were about to come to an end and the next steps had to be weighed carefully since it was now the realities of life that had to be reckoned with.

Having been brought up a good Catholic boy I was a product of the 1940s–1950s and well drenched in the thoughts and precepts of that era. Getting a job, marrying, having a family, and making a living were the primary motivations of the majority of young men of that era. Job security was of paramount importance, or so we thought.

The dastardly Korean War seemed to be winding down and even though no peace treaty was signed, 1958 felt somewhat like a time of relative peace. President Dwight Eisenhower was still a hero of the American people and seemed to have things well in hand in maintaining the prospects of peace and prosperity throughout the land.

During the mid-1950s, little-noticed newspaper articles started appearing stating that aid in the form of military advisors was being advanced to South Vietnam. This was presumably to help the South Vietnamese stem the flow of Communism in that region. With the threat of armed conflict becoming more real by the day, the western world, particularly the USA, became more involved in war preparations. Personally, it meant a surprise notice from my local military draft board to inform me that my number would soon be coming up and to expect a call any day. Any thought of continuing an education via graduate school was to be abandoned.

So, what to do? Should I wait for the draft board to call, flee to Canada like some of my contemporaries or make a move to get into a military band? Going to war in Vietnam was an ideology not readily accepted by a large number of Americans, especially males in my age group. We really didn't have a clear notion of why our country was going to war.

Fleeing to Canada seemed a bit complicated and extreme. Since getting drafted with the thought of going into combat was foreign to my nature, I decided to audition for a military band gig. My clarinet chops were pretty good. I had just recently played a recital at Eastman and soloed with the Rochester Civic Orchestra as a performer's certificate recipient.

Having an abundance of confidence, with clarinet and sax in hand I boarded a Greyhound Bus and made my way to Washington, D.C. to give the U.S. Army Band, Pershing's own, no less, the good fortune of my willingness to join their ranks. Needless to say, I was lacking in humility and still hadn't realized that there were qualified and talented others in my chosen craft.

As it turned out I happened along just at the right moment since there was an opening in the clarinet section and the fact that I played saxophone probably was the reason the audition committee decided that I could be of use to the organization.

The high opinion I had of my abilities rapidly came to a screeching halt when I became aware of the seasoned pros in the band and the musicianship standards I was expected to maintain. So, as I stated previously, *pivotal* was certainly the point I was at in April of 1958.

Getting my official acceptance orders admitting me to The U.S. Army Band was a proud moment in my life until I realized with a shock that passing basic training and preparing to be an infantry foot soldier came with the realization that nothing was for sure when wartime is staring one in the face. My drill sergeant at Fort Dix, New Jersey was quick to drive that fact home to me the instant I arrived and showed him my papers.

"What made you think you were getting into the band, buddy boy?" he snarled with a look of consternation. This man was the epitome of your classic drill sergeant. Muscles bulging from every fold in his pristine starched khaki uniform, and you could comb your hair in the glossy reflection from his perfectly polished GI boots. Years of scowling had created tough creases in his otherwise tight forehead and the image was completed by a voice that could rattle your spine as he barked military orders. In short, he had my attention immediately.

I had been at Fort Dix in Company D for less than a week when I received a notice to appear in his office. Fear gripped every nerve in my body as I arrived since I had not the slightest idea of what he had in mind. I was immediately taken aback when in strode this smiling gentleman who bore no resemblance to the hardened soldier I had recently met. Oh no, I thought, I must be in some kind of trouble this is too good to be true.

Musings on a Musical Journey

"O.K. Regni, you fancy yourself a band guy, right? How about you form a little band to accompany Troop D when we march around the drill field?" I had no idea if this was a possibility but eagerly agreed since I plotted in my mind that carrying a clarinet instead of a rifle was a safer and better use of my talents. Little did I realize at the moment that I was going to be carrying both.

Much to my surprise, I was able to round up a trumpeter, who turned out to be a pretty decent player and a trombonist who was a bit ragged but who could deliver a swoop where needed. The nucleus was there so all I had to do was find a drummer. Since we did not have one in Company D, I had to find someone who was able to beat a bass drum in a somewhat steady rhythm to which the troops could march.

I remembered an out-and-out soldier brawl two days earlier, so I decided to approach the toughest soldier in the group, cautiously I might add, since he was able to beat up everyone that dared to come up against him. He was a muscular 6'4" 275-pound African American. Underneath he was a gentle soul, but no one was going to accuse this guy of being out of time, and the fact that he could hit the drum with such force fit the job description perfectly, as I saw it. In addition to that, he would be a handy ally to be friendly with should another brawl erupt.

Now we had the makings of a band, albeit a small one, but nonetheless, one that could give the illusion of a spirited military group. The sergeant even gave us a weekend furlough to go back home to retrieve our instruments. As a further bonus, I was able to convince him that we needed an hour every morning for band rehearsals. These conditions also scored me points with my chosen bandmates.

Saxophone Troubadour

We managed to put together a military-style mix of Dixieland Music that made us the pride of the Fort Dix Parade field. The sergeant couldn't have been happier and the smile on his face when he marched next to us said it all. I swear I witnessed the buttons popping off of his skintight khaki shirt since his chest seemed a foot in front of the rest of his body.

The eight weeks of basic training seemed as though it would never end. My physical body was in the best shape ever but my head was in the worst shape. The sergeant kept me guessing right up to the final day as to whether or not my band orders were valid. He actually had me believing that my next stop was going to be Saigon, Vietnam as an infantry foot soldier.

On the final day of basic training, he again called me into his office and much to my surprise thanked me for the company band and informed me that my band orders were legitimate and that my next stop would be Fort Myer in Arlington, Virginia the home of The U.S. Army Band, Pershing's own!

He mentioned that the reason he didn't tell me sooner about the band assignment was to keep me focused on being a soldier, because after all, I was a member of the U.S. Army first and foremost, a fact which I never forgot. Man! When he told me that the orders were for real I nearly kissed him on the forehead until I thought carefully about the consequences of such an act.

My three years in the Army were a mixture of frustration, joy, and downright boredom. Playing in the band was hardly what I imagined to be great musical thrills. Sitting in the back end of a 20-player clarinet section was not conducive to creative individualism since it was not possible to even hear yourself. By contrast, playing in some

Musings on a Musical Journey

of the smaller jazz groups was very satisfying, even though these opportunities were infrequent.

On other occasions, the workload could be really small so we would sometimes even sit around wondering whether or not to practice our instruments at all. I remember one occasion in particular when the entire week consisted of a two-hour session with a Catholic priest advising us of the wrongfulness of masturbation. What? Four years of music school to prepare for this?

When things got busy, however, there was not much time to think about whacking off. Much of the time was spent at the Tomb of the Unknown Soldier and Andrews Air Force Base, playing for the arrival of foreign dignitaries.

There were also White House social affairs, Arlington National Cemetery events, and a host of gigs playing at monuments around Washington D.C. In addition, our weekly concert series at the now-defunct floating Water Gate barge under the famous Memorial Bridge proved to be popular events.

Some of the most personally memorable events that I participated in were the 1960 inauguration of President John F. Kennedy; the arrivals of Nikita Khrushchev, French President Charles de Gaulle and Prime Minister Fidel Castro at Andrews Air Force Base; the funeral of General George Marshall; saying hello to Jackie and John Kennedy as they waltzed by our five-piece combo at a White House affair; and most sadly at the mass funeral of 16 members of The U.S. Navy Band who died in a mid-air collision off the coast of Brazil.

A particularly interesting assignment was a trip to Fort Churchill, Manitoba, Canada with a five-piece jazz group. At the time this was a remote army base located near the tundra above the Arctic Circle. Its main purpose was to observe Russian rocket activity to prepare us should we be

Saxophone Troubadour

attacked from across the North Pole. Fortunately for us, we went there in May 1960, which was still frigid but nothing like the dangerous fall and winter months.

Being so far north brought 18 hours a day of sunlight and the job consisted of three hours each evening playing jazz in the base nightclub. This schedule afforded us plenty of time to see the wondrous sights of the Hudson Bay in daylight while enjoying the evenings playing jazz when it was still daylight at 1:00 AM. Aside from the hazardous task of getting there and back in Army big belly cargo planes, the job was thoroughly enjoyable and the troops who were stationed there seemed to really appreciate our efforts.

There were many humorous situations that presented themselves while we were on various assignments. One particularly memorable occasion occurred in January 1960. Washington DC is not particularly known for frigid winters; however, this was one of its coldest days on record.

As is typical of military *hurry up and wait* policy this day was especially notable, as we were to play for one of the first wreath-laying ceremonies by a Japanese Prime Minister at the Tomb of the Unknown Soldier since World War II. We were assembled over one hour before the actual ceremony was to begin. Decked out in our bright Army Blues winter uniforms with heavy overcoats, gloves, and pristine white scarves, we were indeed ready to face the challenge of zero degrees Fahrenheit.

What we were not prepared for however was the fact that each of our instruments had no weather protection and therefore were subject to freezing. No matter how much air we individually blew into our instruments no amount of human hot air could compete with these elements. It was simply impossible to maintain the functionality of our instruments, particularly the trumpets and trombones.

Musings on a Musical Journey

When the Band officer in charge was made to realize this, he promptly notified the chain of command that playing the national anthems of the US and Japan, or anything else with frozen instruments could not happen. Trumpet, baritone, and tuba valves needed to be hit with hammers to move them and a mule team would be needed to move a trombone slide.

When word came back from the commanding general the strict and final order was "YOU WILL PLAY"!

Upon hearing this order, we all thought the commander was possibly a descendent of General George Custer and that he was leading us into an impossible-to-win battle. Either that or he intended to start World War III. He had no concept of how the results would sound. When we tried to play the Japanese National Anthem, it sounded like a cacophonous melee between the Marx Brothers and the Three Stooges.

To bring home the full effect of this abomination the band played as a unified tour de Force without holding anything back. I'll never forget the look of amazed contempt when the Japanese prime minister glanced over at us while he was laying the wreath. The squawks and screeches that came forth were beyond description. How we all managed to keep straight faces through this could only be attributed to our dedicated and unified determination to stick it to the general. The daggers that flowed back to us from the general's eyes when we finished had us horror-stricken and we all knew the consequences were not going to be pretty.

With the ceremony concluded and the prime minister back in the limousine, the general immediately hurried back to the band formation and with every four-letter word ever conceived gave us a major tongue-thrashing. It would have been funnier than the anthem performance except for the fact that he made us stand in formation in the frigid environment for another hour. It all could have been a comedic scene from the TV show Stalag 17.

The punch line came when the obsessively bullying General gave us the order to report on the following morning to the base commissary. Here we were ordered to place our instruments in the meat freezer for two hours before attempting to play them to prove that instruments could not be played in a frozen state. From that day to this, when I hear the oxymoron *Military Intelligence* my memory reverts back to that cold January day in 1960.

There were many days when making music in the Army, however, was a pleasant experience. We were honored to have the well-known pop singer Steve Lawrence as part of the band for two years. I was fortunate to be one member of a small backup group that worked with him on many occasions.

The actual engagements were great but getting to them and back home again was far short of enjoyable and were often downright scary. Because we were at the mercy of weekend air force reserve pilots, the trips were not designed to be comfortable for the passengers. Getting to the destination as quickly as possible was the main priority.

Since they were Air Force reserve pilots fulfilling their remaining tours of duty as civilians, they were in a hurry to get back home to their families. This often meant that going through a storm was necessary if it meant saving an hour or two.

On one such terrifying trip, the chap sitting next to Mr. Lawrence couldn't hold it in and up-chucked with most of the slime hitting Steve and his neatly pressed uniform. Enduring a ride that had us going sideways at times, the poor singer had to sit with this abominable smear all over him. When we finally hit calm weather Steve was able to get a fresh uniform change before returning to his seat. In inimitable Steve Lawrence's good-natured humor, he remarked to the poor sick man "That's a good act you do man. What are you going to do for an encore, shit on me?"

Steve was a wonder, and his quick humor always kept the mood lighthearted. Even in the most nerve-racking situations, he managed to keep us all laughing with one joke after another. Aside from the fact that he was one of the all-time great male singers he was a down-to-earth, kind, humble "one of the guys".

Probably my best experience from my Army days was playing in an off-duty group that was led by the legendary trombonist/arranger Sammy Nestico. Good fortune again came my way when the opening for a jazz tenor sax chair opened up in Sammy's octet. For the better part of three years, I played weekend gigs with his band usually at Bolling Air Force Base.

On Friday nights we played in the service club, Saturday nights in the Non-Commissioned officers' club, and often on Sunday evening in the Officers' club. These gigs were the joy of a lifetime in playing with top players as well as learning from Sammy's genius. On many occasions, he would present us with a new arrangement to add to his library of charts which we considered to be masterpieces. These were Nestico's pre-Count-Basie and Hollywood days when he was honing all of his wonderful writing yet to come. Those were the most memorable times and remain among my greatest joys in making music.

I often reflect on my army days with an attitude of "What's not to like?" Military life was good to me. I happened to be in the right place at the right time on several occasions and met some of the most colorful characters one could ever want to meet. I managed to escape the horrors of war on the front lines but am grateful that I had a drill sergeant

Saxophone Troubadour

who taught me the basics and the honor of being a soldier. Lessons that have proven valuable in life.

Musings on a Musical Journey

Chapter 4
Moving to New York and Getting Started, 1961

It was September 1961 when my first wife, Charlotte, and I set out for the *Big Apple* intending to knock the big time for a loop. Little did we know at the time that it was going to be the other way around for a while. We had heard of *paying your dues* but getting to experience the full brunt of that can only be felt by being there and *drinking the water,* as they say.

Like so many remembrances of past events, my first professional call in the big time, *New York City* was a great memory although it had a dramatic adventure attached.

My wife and I had just barely moved into our East 76th Street apartment when on a Saturday night in September 1961 the phone rang around 9 pm. "Al, it's George, get your alto sax, clarinet, and flute and get over here to the St. George Hotel in Brooklyn, pronto! One of the sax players got sick at the last moment and we need you to get here ASAP," George gasped.

George Marge, who passed away in 1985 was my mentor and the best friend I ever had. We were very much like brothers and would often look out for one another. George was responsible for many contacts that were made for me during my NY career.

Saxophone Troubadour

He would recommend me often. And because he was so highly respected by so many contractors in a variety of musical fields George's recommendations were held in high esteem.

Additionally, the coaching that George gave me about dealing with the business end of the music scene was invaluable. It was clear to me, right from the start, that everyone needs a friend to get one's career off of the ground. This was especially true in a place like New York.

Somewhere around 9:05 pm on that memorable evening, I found my tuxedo which, until then, was still with my unpacked belongings. In a nervous panic, I managed to throw on my tux, find my instruments, check to see that the required reeds for my horns were in place, and flew out the door to the corner of East 76th Street and Third Avenue where I was lucky to get a cab immediately.

Once inside the cab I nervously called out "St George Hotel please!" The typical New York cab driver replete with his New York accent and mild attitude replied, "What's the address?"

"Are you asking me?" I retorted, "I don't even know where Brooklyn is, and least of all how to get there." I had never been to Brooklyn in my life and all I knew is that it was located somewhere east of the East River.

The cab driver turned around and nervously announced that he didn't take Brooklyn calls and said, "Sorry bub, you'll have to get someone else to get you there." After some desperate pleading with him, he finally relented and agreed to give me a hand.

This, incidentally, was my first experience in finding that real New Yorkers will often bend over backward to help out someone needy, even cab drivers. This chap was quick to admit that he had no idea where the Saint George Hotel

Musings on a Musical Journey

was. Either that or he saw it as an opportunity to make a few extra bucks by taking me on a bonus ride.

After a moment or two of checking his Brooklyn map, he found it and realized it was in Brooklyn Heights and a fairly short distance from the famous Brooklyn Bridge. Looking at the map, it seemed like it was very accessible and not going to be difficult to locate. I breathed a huge sigh of relief when we zipped down the East River Drive in just a few minutes from our starting point and exited at the Brooklyn Bridge in what seemed like record time.

The typical thing about New York cab drivers is that they love it when there is a crisis or any excuse to break speed laws. This hack was no different and he had me white-knuckling right onto the huge, curved exit ramp at the foot of the bridge. That cab ride compounded my anxiety and made me wonder if I would even get to the Saint George Hotel in one piece. This was not the way I wished to remember or relish my first trip across that famous landmark.

So here we are, my first experience traveling into the borough of Brooklyn with all of the attached excitement plus the exhilaration of flying low in a taxi and the anticipation of my first New York gig. Now, all we had to do was find the hotel which was probably less than two miles from our Brooklyn Bridge exit.

Anyone who has gone through the maze of the beginning steps of navigating a computer knows that the initial learning process requires much-focused trial and error. Finding one's way around the complicated layout of Brooklyn streets is much the same as the patience required with computers and cannot be rushed. We did not have that mindset and the fact that we were so close and yet so far compounded my anxiety.

Saxophone Troubadour

After a good half an hour of exploring the neighborhood, we finally found our destination. My relief was suddenly interrupted when the cabbie announced that the fare was going to be at the reduced rate of $15.00. He was kind enough to knock off some of the cost because of the circuitous route we took.

In 1961, that was considered an enormous fare. I'm sure that in 2020 the cost would have been at least $50.00. My shock at discovering that I only had $11.00 in my wallet was the next crisis. I now had to figure out how to get the remaining dollars to pay the fare and add a tip. I had to find my friend George!

I convinced the driver to give me a few minutes by leaving my precious Martin alto saxophone with him as collateral. I took a last look and said a prayer as I exited the cab and hoped that it was not the last time that I would see that beautiful gold lacquered instrument. I left the cab double-parked on Brooklyn Heights' narrow Henry Street, in the loading zone of the hotel, I hurriedly made my way into the main entrance.

Since I was nervous that the driver couldn't sit double-parked for very long, I blindly scurried into the main entrance past exquisitely uniformed doormen and through the enormous lavish lobby. After many wrong turns in the maze of nooks and crannies of several ballrooms, I somehow found the gigantic main ballroom.

The Saint George Hotel, in its heyday, was the largest and among the most elegant of New York City hotels. Established in 1885, it remained a lush landmark structure until the late 1960s when it fell into difficult times and became severely rundown. It was best known during the pre-World War II era for being a playground for celebrities such as F. Scott Fitzgerald, Johnny Weissmuller of Tarzan fame, and a host of Hollywood luminaries. It featured a saltwater 120-foot swimming pool, over 2,632 guest rooms, and was capable of accommodating seven thousand diners at any one time. The Grand Ballroom boasted an open floor that would provide enough space for 3000 dancers. The bar room was also the location for some famous filming of *The Godfather* movie. I was completely in awe of the grandeur of this venue.

The event in progress was the first big banquet/dance fundraiser for the St. Jude Hospital of Memphis, Tennessee. The legendary founder, comedian/actor Danny Thomas was in attendance as were an overwhelming number of Hollywood celebrities, famous sports figures, political luminaries, and others. There was a familiar face everywhere. Danny Thomas must have had enormous clout to obtain the presence and support of so many people of importance. It rivaled the Academy Awards in its degree of glitz.

After gaining entrance to this auspicious display of luxury, I managed to weave my way through a crowd of couples dancing to the music of Eddie, *The Sheik* Kochak's band, known for a mixture of various music styles and ethnicities.

Mr. Thomas was of Lebanese descent, so people danced to a mixture of American pop music and Eastern European melodies. It was an interesting mélange of music but an extremely high level of professionalism on all fronts. It was exciting to be exposed to a first-class New York event with a band of 22 top pros putting out a great variety of sounds. The Sheik was rotating between playing an Egyptian drum called a Doumbek on the Lebanese selections and fronting the orchestra like a 1940s swing bandleader on the American repertoire.

Since it was my first exposure to such a display it was very exciting even though I was a nervous wreck thinking

Saxophone Troubadour

about an unknown New York cabbie disappearing with my prized Martin Alto Saxophone. I waited patiently, biting my tongue to shreds, while the band finished the number they were playing.

The Sheik was counting off the next tune with 2000 dancers waiting when I ran up onto the stage and found George. I felt like I had reached the summit of Mt. McKinley when I got to him and blurted out "George loan me 10 bucks fast."

Before he could open his wallet, I grabbed it and flew off the stage. Out of the corner of my eye, I observed the incredulous stare coming from the noble leader who was probably thinking, "who is this maniac?"

The relief was overwhelming when I arrived back at the taxi and found the driver snoozing right where I left him. In the back seat was my treasure waiting for me. I was so delirious I gave the man an extra $15.00. George wouldn't mind, after all this was an emergency and I thought this saintly man did me a huge favor that was worth a respectable tip. It was respectable in the days when I had no money.

Arriving back to the bandstand I got to my seat next to good friend George and joyfully played my part. It was the beginning of a lifelong adventure that never seemed to end. To this day I'm amazed that I got paid and was able to make a living having such a good time.

We got to NYC with two cars, big mistake #1, from Arlington, Virginia, and immediately found that having a car in Manhattan is not only a luxury but a huge pain in the ass. One either has the funds to pay exorbitant garage fees or has the patience to spend many hours driving around countless street blocks looking for non-existent parking places. Consequently, our priority was to get rid of one of the cars—ultimately to get rid of both.

Musings on a Musical Journey

Parting with our two-toned blue 1956 Studebaker President, Limited Edition was like tearing off one of my arms. It sported light and dark blue plush upholstered seats with clear seat covers and a globe speedometer that sat atop the dash. I was about to lose my best friend. Selling it in New York without a trade-in on a new car was next to impossible in those days. Studebakers were on the way out and we would have had a better chance of selling a bob-sled in the Gobi Desert.

Two days of visiting every used car dealer in the city proved to be utterly useless so the next plan was to scour Long Island starting in Astoria Queens. This proved to be a virgin experience in acquainting ourselves with every shyster in the area. It was open season on two wet-behind-the-ears newcomers. One guy even offered to take the car off of our hands if I paid him! Drive on we did and proceeded to get our early lessons in developing the hard skin and arrogant demeanor of seasoned New Yorkers.

Finally, after another few days, we ended up in the far reaches of Long Island in a town whose name I still do not know. Here we found a nice used car salesman who gave us the unforgivable sum of $25.00 for the car. How could I resist this pleasant, kind smiling gentleman?

This turned out to be another lesson in how to get ripped-off New York style. I would have shed a few tears were it not for the fact that finding our way back to our East 76th Street Manhattan apartment was disastrous. We had to take the Long Island Railroad, a bus, and the NY Subway. Lesson number two in developing the critically necessary New York attitude: returning to our tiny two-room apartment which was approximately the size of my present wife Rosy's walk-in closet, was depressing, to say the least, but a step in the direction of becoming hardened natives.

Saxophone Troubadour

Our apartment was approximately 700 square feet including one bathroom, a kitchen, and two 12-foot rooms. The entrance went into the kitchen which allowed room for two people but room for only one to cook. The bathroom was off the kitchen and a bit annoying for both the person working in the kitchen and the one needing to go to the john.

The paper-thin walls did not make for good neighbor relations due to my incessant practicing but somehow, we managed to co-exist peacefully. The tiny living room was packed with a sofa, one easy chair, and a TV set. Everything else in that minuscule area had to be hung on the walls.

The second room was one that is hard to describe. It held a double bed smack in the middle of the room, a dining table, an upright piano, two dressers, and a desk. There were approximately 12 inches of walking space in that minefield. Getting up in the middle of the night to go to the bathroom was like walking a tightwire at the circus. The one closet we shared had to hold every bit of clothing we owned. I tell you all of this because just living in the city is one more lesson in gaining that signature NY attitude.

Now we needed the funds to just survive, one of the many nightmares of everyone who moves to New York City. We came to the city with the few bucks we had saved up but it was a pittance compared to what was needed just to pay the rent and eat. I was going to school earning a master's degree and picking up an odd job here and there.

Fortunately, my wife Charlotte obtained a *real* job in a Madison Avenue advertising agency, and were it not for that we probably would have had to make an early retreat. She had a finely trained soprano voice, and also was quick to get a job singing in a very good East Side church with some excellent NY voices. Strangely enough, they were pretty happy days. It was exciting, and we were able to cultivate quite a few friends. We lived from hand to mouth for the first couple of years but somehow believed that it was just a matter of time before things would go our way.

Working in the city as a newcomer was not an easy task so I was relegated to finding work on the road with a variety of the big bands of the day. Among the bands that I worked with were Tommy Dorsey, Les and Larry Elgart, Richard Maltby, and Warren Covington. They all turned out to be valuable musical and life experiences.

After a couple of years of doing road gigs, I found that it was not something I could sustain for very long with any hope of keeping a normal life. I didn't realize at the time the experience of going on the road with the big-name bands was a good education in more ways than one. Traveling mostly in the Southeast in the early 1960s gave insights that lasted a lifetime.

Jim Crow was still a big part of the country's mindset. It was definitely a different lifestyle than what I experienced growing up in the bergs of up-state New York. Playing with the name bands, however, was great in many ways and a story worth telling.

My first post-road trip, steady job was at a nightclub in Forest Hills, Queens. This was in 1963 and it was in many ways a dream gig. The name of the venue was The Carlton Terrace, and it was a classy place, albeit a *cheater's club*. This was a trysting spot for the 1960s sex-thirsty married folks who were looking for a bit of action on the side.

Personally though, it was something that I had hoped for from a musical standpoint since it was a quartet made up of some really fine musicians. The group consisted of the leader, an excellent pianist named Mike Vasallo; he was always tastefully dressed and groomed and looked every bit the part of a slick New York orchestra leader. If I ever had

Saxophone Troubadour

to cast the part of a bandleader in a Hollywood movie Mike would have been my man.

The upright Bass player was a handsome young man who was a magnet for the ladies dancing by. The third member of the quartet was a fine drummer with classic Italian looks and who dressed as if he had just arrived from the Milan, Italy fashion industry. He sported a well-groomed pencil-thin mustache and was a perfect fit for a re-making of the classic Italian movie *Big Deal on Madonna Street*. And last, there was me on the reeds. All-in-all a darned good-looking band who managed to sound pretty good, as well.

The working conditions were more than fine, the boss treated us very respectfully, we played quality music and most importantly the pay was good and always on time. I should add that the job was well-timed as it allowed us to move to a larger more upscale apartment in the better positioned upper west side of Manhattan. It was easier to move around in the territory where most of the work for the music business was located, i.e. Broadway, recording studios, etc.

Now things were shaping up beautifully. At last, my wife and I had steady jobs and nice new living conditions with wonderful neighbors. I was playing interesting music, mostly Jazz and Latin, getting to play all of my instruments including sax, clarinet, and flute on a good level. In short, I was a happy camper.

I should mention that the hours for the job were from 8 pm to 1 am, six nights a week. Getting home at 2:00 am and then having to find a parking place in the wee small hours was the hardest part of the job. That was okay as the gig made it all worthwhile, until Friday, November 22, 1963!

On that day at 12:30 pm our beloved president, John Fitzgerald Kennedy was assassinated. For those of us who were around at the time, it was a day when we all fell into total shock. For me, it came a few hours after I was nearly mugged while walking back to our apartment at 2:30 am on November 22nd, after cruising the streets looking for a parking space.

    I finally found a spot behind the Cathedral of St. John Divine near West 110th Street. It was a place that was hidden, out-of-the-way, very dark, and the perfect place for a mugging. Two sinister-looking guys came toward me with every inch of their body language saying that I was going to be their next victim. I was carrying a clarinet, tenor saxophone, and a pricy flute, all uninsured. These were the only tools of my profession that I owned and I was not going to part with them without a fight.

    As the two thugs crossed the street and headed straight toward me, I intuitively switched all the horns to one side of my body and reached into my pocket as if I was carrying a weapon. In 1963 this was a good move. In today's world, I probably wouldn't be around to tell this tale.

    The ploy worked and the two muggers did an about-face and walked back across the street. Of course, I was a bit shaken. For the rest of the trek back to the apartment I started rethinking what I was doing. Did I want to continue this lifestyle or was it time to re-think my life's path?

    Tragically the next few hours would give me a clear answer to that question. I'll never forget the disruption to the peace and tranquility of my lunch after the harrowing episode of a few hours earlier. The beautiful music on the local radio station was halted by the voice of Walter Cronkite whose somber words recounted the events of President Kennedy's assassination. A half-hour later at 2 pm, the official announcement came that the president had died.

    The stunning news left a cloud of numbness over our entire country as well as the rest of the world. New York

Saxophone Troubadour

immediately closed: stores closed, Broadway closed, restaurants closed, in short, the world came to a screeching halt, every place except the Carlton Terrace. I couldn't believe my ears when I was told that the nightclub would be open. I was reminded that Friday night was pick-up night and that simply could not be postponed.

When I learned we were going to be playing that night a bolt hit that gave me a shock of profound disbelief. The shock was further intensified as I realized that the festivities were proceeding as if it were just another night of frivolity. At the end of the first set and just before our usual 15-minute break, I turned to our leader Mike and said, "Please have someone here tomorrow night because this is it for me."

It was sad that it took such a tragic event for me to come to this decision but as it turned out it was one of the best moves I ever made. Seeing the look on my wife's face when I told her I had quit my job was not pretty. "You did what?", she retorted in disbelief. Here we were just starting to get things rolling and I was back to square one, or so it seemed.

Funny how fate sometimes can pave an unexpected path. It was not very long after my knee-jerk reaction of departing from The Carlton Terrace that the telephone rang, and I was called to sub at Radio City Music Hall. Several months earlier, I had interviewed there for some work and I had begun to think that it was a lost cause. That call was certainly a pleasant thing that not only took me by surprise but more importantly proved to be an excellent source of professional contacts.

Having the exposure to display one's work is a very important piece in the puzzle of success in any industry. The music business is no different since the opportunities are not always present and when they are it's very

Musings on a Musical Journey

important to meet the challenge by being well prepared. There have been many occasions when the timing is right, but the performer is not. There are very few overnight sensations and for most of them, the process requires a combination of luck, readiness, exposure, patience, good human relations, and total commitment.

My first chance at gaining some attention came when I was asked to play the E-flat Clarinet solo in Ravel's Bolero at Radio City Music Hall. When the call came in, I didn't even own an E-flat clarinet but that wasn't going to cause me to pass up this opportunity. This was a real chance to shine and get some attention. The conductor at that time was the legendary Raymond Paige of Hollywood fame.

In those days the Music Hall had a format of four live 45-minute stage shows with a lavish 90-piece orchestra. The shows were at 12 noon, 3 pm, 6 pm, and 9 pm and interspersed with a feature film. I had two days to get myself an E-flat clarinet and my youthful fearlessness led me to believe it would be an easy task. Little did I know! After a couple of telephone calls, I found that I could obtain an instrument that was German-made and seemed to fit the need perfectly. Added to that, it only cost $100 and I thought this was too good to be true.

When I got the instrument home, I found it was quite a different story as the instrument was horribly out of tune and in short, a total disaster. I spent the better part of one whole day trying to figure out how to make the horn sound presentable by making up a whole new set of fingerings to accommodate the sad state of this poor excuse for a musical instrument.

Through some miracle, I made it through the first show at noon on the following day with a modicum of success and a maximum of sweat and terror. When I showed the instrument to the first clarinetist Bob Listokin, I can still

Saxophone Troubadour

hear him saying "This ain't a German clarinet, this is a Nazi clarinet."

That was it! I now had approximately two hours and no money to get an instrument that would get me through and preserve my chances at a professional career in New York City.

Back in the 1960s and well into the 1990s the music street was West 48th Street between Sixth and Seventh Avenues. The Street consisted of a plethora of music stores known as Music Row. Some of the many shops were Charlie Ponte Music, Rudy's, New York Music Company, Manny's, Alex's, Terminal, and many more.

The one that many reed players preferred was Linx and Long. This store was a virtual institution of musical higher learning. Being there at any time would place you in the presence of a mix of great musicians. At one counter you might see Dizzy Gillespie with half of Count Basie's band, at another, an assortment of players from the Metropolitan Opera or the New York Philharmonic. Great musical sounds would be emanating from the adjoining studios with everything from a woodwind quartet to virtuoso soloists. It was nothing less than thrilling just to walk into the place.

Dashing out of Radio City at the corner of West 50th Street and Sixth Avenue I made my way to Linx and Long and fortunately for me, the owner Jack Linx was behind the counter. He was not busy when I arrived which was a rarity. There was usually a half-hour wait at least to get to see him. I explained my dilemma to Jack emphasizing the need for a fine quality Eb Clarinet and also explaining I had no money.

I did have an instrument to trade in. I should have said to trash and pleaded with him to sell me a new Selmer that he happened to have in the showcase on display. Even though I had no money at that moment I pleaded with Jack

Musings on a Musical Journey

to take my trade-in with the promise that I would have the money to him by the next week.

Jack was a pleasant easy-going man, short, pleasingly plump, and always sporting a smile. With a look of pity on his face, he could sense my desperation and I often think about how he saved my career at that moment. He knew what it was like to get started in the music business in New York City and was willing to give me a break. It also helped that I was one of his regular customers purchasing all of my accessories from him. If I had to play another exposed solo on that poor excuse for an instrument it would have been goodbye to that gig. I got the instrument and promised Mr. Linx I would have the money for him by the end of the week, which I did.

The 3 pm performance went great, and I was a hit with Maestro Paige. He gave me a big smile and a thumbs up which made me feel like I had made the *big time*. Having a first-rate instrument gave me the confidence of a seasoned pro even though I was not. There's something to say for New York chutzpah and I put it all out there at that moment. It was a first step at getting some well-needed exposure. As in any business, the opportunity to get heard or noticed is not always readily available and I was not only lucky to have that chance but was equally fortunate to have it pay off. From then on I was always rewarded with a big smile from Mr. Paige and had several opportunities to play solos for him on future occasions.

A humorous side note: a while after the Linx and Long store went out of business I ventured out to Hillsdale, New Jersey to the home of Nick Engleman, the saxophone repairman who was a staple of the Linx and Long family. When the shop closed, many of Nick's customers, including me, would travel out to his home where he had a nifty woodwind repair room in his basement.

Saxophone Troubadour

He worked at an antique roll-top desk which held every tool of woodwind repair known to man. He was a wise soul who had dealt with the best musicians on the scene and had many tales to tell. His specks always slid down on his nose and he had the sage look of a man well-schooled in human relations. Sitting on top of the desk was a very familiar piece of personal memorabilia. Here sat the remains of what Bob Listokin labeled my "Nazi" E-flat clarinet and which now had been turned into an out-of-tune table lamp.

Radio City was a great place in those days not only for being a good job but also a place that was a stepping stone to work on Broadway and the New York recording studios. For me, it was not only that, but it provided me a contact that would serve me well for the next 50 years of my NY career.

My work at Radio City was as a substitute for a couple of the reed players. One day I might sub for the solo clarinetist while another day one of the inside reed books. My main sub was for the lead Alto Sax book that was the job of a musician named Gregory Raffa. Gregg was a busy man as the manager of Plaza Sound, the recording studio on the sixth floor of the Radio City building. In addition to being a smooth businessman, he was the main first reed player with a contract for 16 shows a week, and his regular alternate would be contracted for the remaining eight shows a week.

Gregg, being ultra-busy with the recording studio plus an abundance of other outside work would call me regularly to sub for him two days a week or eight shows. So even though it was a definite maybe, I could usually count on going in for him every Tuesday and Thursday. Since I was the new kid on the block I was at his disposal and at this stage of the game, happy to be.

Musings on a Musical Journey

July 9, 1963 was a Tuesday that went down as a personally memorable day. Since I was subbing for Gregg on that day, I had just finished doing the noon show and was relaxing in the musician's lounge. The old saying of being in the right place at the right time had proved true on that day. Usually, right after the noon show, the routine would be to head out to get lunch. For some reason on that particular day, I decided to hang out in the lounge for a while and thus was the only one there when the public phone rang. Since I was alone, I answered. Gregg's voice came on, "Al I'm glad I caught you, can you do a gig for me tomorrow morning with the New York Philharmonic?"

I thought I was dreaming and before he could finish the question I blurted out, "Oh yes."

"They're doing Leonard Bernstein's *On the Waterfront* and it's got a nice Alto Sax solo, have you ever done it?"

My fabricated answer was yes, even though I had only seen and heard the movie score, but was not about to let this opportunity pass me by. As soon as I hung up the phone and picked myself up off the floor I made a mad dash for Patelson's Music Store which was located on West 56th St across from the stage door of Carnegie Hall.

Patelson's was a famous sheet music store at the time. In the days before the internet, they were one of the world's great shops for finding copies of solo pieces for every instrument as well as a large selection of orchestral scores. Whenever there was time to spare, Patelson's was the place for musicians to be, just to peruse the wealth of music on the shelves and the record store in the rear of the shop.

It didn't take long to find the orchestral score to "On the Waterfront" as well as the original recording with Leonard Bernstein conducting the New York Philharmonic. I was excited beyond belief and couldn't wait to finish the 9 pm

Saxophone Troubadour

show so I could get home and pour myself into learning the sax part.

I must have stayed up until 4 am because sleep was not a priority. The coming rehearsal at Lewisohn Stadium at 10 am on West 138th Street was only a few hours away. Things went very well at the rehearsal and the concert. After I got over the initial rookie jitters, I felt very good about having taken another stepping stone in the right direction in my New York career.

Musings on a Musical Journey

Chapter 5
Broadway to Texas and Back, 1963 – 2002

Playing on Broadway has always been a highly sought-after job on the New York music scene in that it provided many perks in addition to steady employment. Since most musicians kept track of who was doing what show at any given time it was a way to become known and gain a foothold in the industry.

Doing Broadway was also a means to some financial security with a pension fund and various health benefits attached. Many musicians sought Broadway as a subsidy to other preferred free-lance activities that were not long-term financially endowed.

It took a couple of years of beating the pavement, but I got my first break to play a Broadway show in 1963. The show was *Bajour* and starred the fabulous Chita Rivera. It was a baptism of fire because it was an involved clarinet book along with flute and alto saxophone. The music was technically challenging with fast and furious Gypsy licks. It even had a section for a featured jazz flute solo which I looked forward to playing at every performance.

I entered the show after it had been running for several months as a replacement for a player who had moved on to another show. Getting one's own show usually involved a process of being a sub while the regular player took off for

Saxophone Troubadour

vacation or other engagements. If the regular left the show permanently, the sub would take over full time as a replacement. Step three was to graduate to becoming hired as an original band member. This was a big step. Starting in the orchestra of an original Broadway show was a rite of passage toward being labeled a New York pro.

I wasn't there yet but I could feel the time was near. *Bajour* was exciting in several ways, mostly because I sat next to legendary French hornist Arthur Berv. Mr. Berv had a luminous career as solo principal French Horn with the NBC Symphony under Arturo Toscanini as well as principal horn with the Philadelphia Orchestra and several other major orchestras. He was a very distinguished gentleman with a captivating treasure trove of experiences.

I loved hearing about them during the many little dialogue breaks in the show. I would sit in awe and wonderment as he related what it was like to play for the likes of Arturo Toscanini, Otto Klemperer, and a host of international legendary conductors.

Unfortunately, *Bajour* only lasted another five weeks from the date that I joined the orchestra. But it was sweet while it lasted, I was back out on the street again doing subs to keep my toes in the water and pay the bills. During that time, I was becoming known around town as a reliable substitute and managed to work in several shows before landing another permanent replacement in the giant hit *Funny Girl*.

This was the hottest show in town at the time, especially since it featured the superstar, Barbra Streisand. Being on a regular payroll meant not only a steady good salary but the start of a pension fund and health benefits which was a giant relief. Another perk was the fact that I could move around on a couple of other woodwind chairs within *Funny Girl* at various times to get experience on other instruments such as flute, alto flute, piccolo, and alto saxophone. My regular job in the show was as clarinetist and tenor saxophonist.

Funny Girl with its fabulous score by Jule Styne and arrangements by Ralph Burns ran for a total of three years which made it a mega-hit in the 1960s. Alongside long-running shows such as *Oklahoma*, *Showboat*, and *My Fair Lady* it was one of only a few big musical productions of the day that ran three years or longer.

When *Funny Girl* closed in July of 1967, I heard the news with a combination of fear and relief. I had become accustomed to a steady paycheck on one hand, but the boredom of doing eight shows a week was a reason to reconsider my growth as a musician. Maintaining the skills to play the somewhat demanding parts in an eight-performance a week show and keeping a fresh approach to creativity was conflicting.

Since I had begun doing work at the New York Philharmonic, the Metropolitan Opera, and the New York City Ballet I was beginning to feel the strain of wearing different hats and having to perform on high levels in different musical environments. Broadway was still the job that offered a secure future monetarily, but the other areas were more desirable for artistic realization. Since I loved them all, there was no way that I was about to give up on any one of these amazing opportunities.

When *Funny Girl* closed, I was again terrified about making a living. All of the benefits of a steady paycheck were constantly on my mind. It was an enormous relief when the phone rang and to my surprise, the voice of tyrannical New York musical contractor Morris Stonzek was on the other end offering a job as the first reed player in a new Broadway show *Mata Hari*. The show was originally scheduled for a three-week try-out in Washington DC at the

Saxophone Troubadour

National Theatre followed by a month in Philadelphia at the Schubert Theatre. Because it was such a big production there was also a likelihood of additional tryouts in New Haven, Connecticut. I was not thrilled at the need to be out of town for such a long time but the thought of an extended period of lucrative paychecks was an enormous comfort in that our child was about to be born.

Mata Hari was the story of the infamous World War I spy who was eventually executed by a French firing squad. This show was expected to be the hit of the day and Broadway's most prominent producer David Merrick brought along Pernell Roberts who left his hit TV show *Bonanza* to take on the leading role.

The part of Mata Hari was played by newcomer Marisa Mell. Ms. Mell was an extraordinarily beautiful Austrian actress, who was inexperienced at big Broadway musicals. Two additional problems were that she couldn't sing and didn't speak English.

Vincente Minnelli of Hollywood notoriety was the original director. He had become famous for having directed many blockbusters such as *An American in Paris* and *Gigi*. It was apparent that he was out of his element when it came to Broadway, however. An obvious hint came as his first words at the opening rehearsal were, "OK, roll 'em." This was an appropriate term for a movie director, but a no-no for sensitive Broadway people.

Mata Hari was and still is to date one of the biggest flops in Broadway history. The show received such scathing reviews from every critic that Mr. Merrick came on stage after the final curtain of the opening preview to give an oral whiplashing to the entire crew on the disaster he had just witnessed. It is said that he lost $500,000 on one opening preview performance production alone.

Musings on a Musical Journey

The most memorable part of the show for me personally was driving on weekend car trips back to New York City when Blythe Danner would hitch a ride and make for some pleasant company. She had a supporting role in the show and although it was her first big-time gig it was apparent that she held the promise of future stardom.

Although *Mata Hari* was a total disaster, several humorous incidents went down in the annals of Broadway's all-time hilarious blooper history. Opening night started with the orchestra conductor appearing decked out in white tie and tails and promptly poking himself in the nose with his baton. This while giving an excessively effervescent upbeat to the overture. He couldn't have hit a more exact bull's-eye, or should I say bull's-nose. He seemed to lose half of the length of the baton up his left nostril.

The entire overture consisted of a combination of our leader's attempt to conduct and give cues with one hand while stemming the flow of blood that was streaming from his nose. This was followed by numerous set disasters that either failed to get to the stage on time or only partially appeared.

One of the sets was of an elaborate three-story Swiss chalet whose second deck contained Mister Roberts. The set only made it to about one-third of its on-stage appearance, leaving the star to sing his big production number behind the curtain. It was probably just as well since the tune was pretty lame.

Dropped lines as well as misplaced or dropped stage articles plagued the entire performance but tragically the most humorous incident saved itself for the end of the show. *Mata Hari* had just been executed by a firing squad, the stage lighting was not operating properly, while the final tear-jerking song had just been sung.

Saxophone Troubadour

Mata Hari had been executed and was hanging slumped over the post where she was tied for an excruciatingly long period. Nothing was happening on a dark stage and the eerie delay was an embarrassment to everyone in the theatre. Poor *Mata Hari* (Marisa Mell), bent over in an awkward position, had an itch on her nose which was more than she could bear. The lights came on just as she scratched, but she supposedly had been shot dead. The entire audience broke out into hilarious laughter, all except David Merrick, of course.

The most tragic moment of the production was instantly turned into a comedic scene that even a Mel Brooks or *Saturday Night Live* routine could not surpass. Mr. Merrick's veins were popping from his neck and we all suspected, rather knew, at that moment, that this show was now definitely doomed. Just to add to everyone's embarrassment, the First Lady of the land, Lady Bird Johnson was sitting up front with distinguished members of the Democratic Women's Convention.

A four-month out-of-town try-out plus an anticipated long New York run was suddenly reduced to three weeks of rehearsal and one preview performance that took me back to New York and unemployment. This was a bit worrisome as our child was about to be born. The big takeaway from the show was the name Marisa which was new to me at the time and made such an impression that we named our newborn daughter Marissa, adding the "s" to further Anglicize the name.

To my surprise, the phone rang shortly after I arrived back in New York. It was the terrifying personnel orchestra manager, Morris Stonzek. He was very intimidating to Broadway musicians as he had been known to blackball players for any number of reasons. He was the most powerful contractor at the time and because of this he was nicknamed *The Pope*.

We all wanted to stay on his good side and after the *Mata Hari* disaster, I feared he would never call me again. His appearance reminded me of Dr. Thaddeus Sivana, the snaky, squint-eyed supervillain of the *Captain Marvel* comic book fame. To my surprise, he did offer me another pre-Broadway show called *The Fig Leaves Are Falling* with music by Albert Hague and lyrics written by a pop star of the day named, Allan Sherman. It featured the current teen idol, David Cassidy. We did a month of turbulent try-outs at the Schubert Theatre in Philadelphia. *Fig Leaves* at least made it to New York but the show was savaged by the New York critics and promptly closed after only five performances. I was starting to think that all I was being hired to play in were flops.

I was pleasantly surprised again when "the Pope" called and offered me a show called *The Happy Time* which was scheduled to open a couple of weeks later at the Broadway theatre. It was written by the duo of John Kander and Fred Ebb and featured the popular vocalist, Robert Goulet. The slick choreography was created by the famous Gower Champion who also directed the show. It lasted nine months and was thoroughly enjoyable in every way. *The Happy Time* was a delightful gig, with a wonderful cast, terrific band, and very pleasant people to work with. It ran during the time of the birth of my daughter Marissa, so it was indeed a happy period personally.

By the end of *The Happy Time*, I had established a fairly good connection or *grapevine* as they say, and was getting many calls to do Broadway sub-work. In a way that was better than having a regular steady show because I was free to keep my extra work at the NY Phil, The Metropolitan Opera, and The NY City Ballet going. After all, these were my preferred gigs, and I was happiest musically at these venues.

The downside was that my union health, welfare, and pension payments were not as good as the Broadway contract, so it was a little more tenuous from the financial and welfare aspect. By the end of the 1960s, I was beginning to feel a sense of security in that there were several areas where I was able to work. In addition to the live gigs, I was beginning to get calls for studio recording work which gave me a feeling of being a true New York freelance woodwind doubler. It was an exciting, busy time for me and the thrill of moving through many of music venues all around the city gave me an increased sense of confidence.

In 1969, a new show came to town called *Coco*. It was a musical based on the life of the famous French fashion designer Coco Chanel. The show brought some wonderful superstars to Broadway headed by the legendary Katherine Hepburn. The music was written by Andre Previn of Hollywood and Symphonic fame, lyricist Alan Jay Lerner, conductor Robert Emmett Dolan, director Michael Bennett and the wonderful orchestrator Hershy Kay.

It was indeed an all-star gathering. Getting a call to be in the reed section of that show was a real honor to me and there was no way I could turn that down. In addition, it was contracted by another powerful New York personnel manager named Sol Gusikoff. Although I had worked a few freelance gigs for Mr. Gusikoff, I was never employed by him to do a prominent chair in a Broadway pit. So, I was not going to say no, even though my aspirations at the time were to get away from Broadway and concentrate on more serious musical pursuits.

After playing the show for less than a year, my musical life sent me an exciting new surprise. A phone call from Joe

Musings on a Musical Journey

DeAngelis, the personnel manager of the New York Philharmonic offered me a way to get back into the kind of music that I enjoyed most. He invited me to join the New York Philharmonic as saxophonist and clarinetist on a tour of Japan which was to take place in August of 1970. This was a most prestigious event which is described in another chapter of this writing.

The problem that arose because of the invitation was a bit challenging in that I had to get permission to leave the show prematurely, both from the music director Robert Emmett Dolan as well as from contractor Sol Gusikoff. This was not an easy task in that the musician's union contract stipulated that the rules for an individual member to leave or to be dismissed were strictly enforced.

In this case, Maestro Dolan was not happy about me wanting to leave the show. While he was a stalwart on the Hollywood scene his New York experience on Broadway was limited and this ended up working to my benefit. It was a fairly common practice for players to seek permission to leave a show, usually to start a new show. Mr. Dolan was very comfortable with the orchestra and did not like the thought of any changes. I knew that *Bobby*, as he was affectionately called, was a very kind and understanding sort so I persisted in an attempt to convince him that I would find him the best replacement in a star pool of New York woodwind players.

After a couple of weeks of pleading and many after-show martinis at a nearby bar, he finally came around and gave me his blessing. The contractor, Sol Gusikoff was so amazed that he invited me to his Lincoln Square apartment for a wonderful lunch with him and his wife, much to my surprise. I think he wanted to know what, if any, tactics I used to convince the conductor to concede and permit me to leave the show. He also couldn't believe that I wanted to leave such an excellent job. Everyone was happy when I was able to secure the well-known virtuoso Charlie Russo to take over the job.

The 1970s was a particularly exciting time. I was hired to be a part of the Bernstein *Mass* which opened the John F. Kennedy Center for the Performing Arts in Washington, D.C. It was August of 1971 when I was one of 10 *ringers* from New York. I traveled to Washington to join a large cast of actors, musicians, singers, and dancers from various parts of the country to be a part of this lavish and somewhat controversial production.

It was composed at the request of Jacqueline Kennedy expressly for the opening of the center. Bernstein's choice of an eclectic version of the Roman Catholic liturgy with influences of the turmoil that was so prevalent in the 1960s created a dramatic tension that was difficult for most audiences to digest, particularly conservative Roman Catholics. At times there would be loud booing and at one performance an angry audience member ran down the center aisle of the J.F. Kennedy Opera House spilling blood which turned out to be tomato juice. Much excitement!!

The production required prolonged rehearsal times, extensive stage preparations, and coordination that was exhausting. We spent the better part of August 1971 in rehearsal for the opening which occurred on September 8, 1971. During this time most of us *Mass* participants were housed in the Holiday Inn which was across from the Watergate Hotel on Virginia Avenue, Northwest.

Being at that lodging then was significant as it was the period when the plans for the famous break-in of the Watergate in 1972 were being formulated. We residents became aware of several shady characters roaming the halls of the hotel and suspected that something was amiss.

Musings on a Musical Journey

It came as no surprise when we learned a couple of months later that the break-ins did indeed occur, and it seemed obvious that the shady characters we had observed were the culprits. We discovered later that they had set up their high-powered cameras in various rooms of the Holiday inn to observe the happenings directly across the street.

In addition to the weirdos, the infamous photographer, Ron Galella was in residence. He was notorious for his obsession with photographing Jacqueline Kennedy. Many mornings while we musicians were having breakfast, Ron would hang around the dining room to get information about our rehearsal schedules for the day. He knew that Jackie was a regular attendee at most scheduled rehearsals so he would plan his positioning strategies accordingly, to photograph her coming and going at the various venues.

All of us band people made a pact and would play a game of giving Mr. Galella the wrong time and locations of the rehearsals in an attempt to throw him off track. He was however too slick a paparazzi to be fooled by amateurs and always seemed to be in the right spot at the precise time that Jackie would be out in the open. He was a supreme pain in the butt but also an expert at his craft. With his notorious obsession for photographing Jackie, he was able to get some fabulous photographs. Eventually, Mrs. Kennedy obtained a restraining order against him.

The *Mass* opened to lukewarm reviews and in my estimation was ahead of its time. Reviewers seemed to mainly criticize its controversial subject with little praise for its artistic content. For me, it was one of the highlights of my days in music as was anything Bernstein composed or conducted.

As a young ambitious sort, I did not consider or was aware enough of the necessary discipline of balance in my life. My focus was becoming more and more preoccupied

Saxophone Troubadour

with becoming one of the best in my field. In one sense it was a noble pursuit but in another, it was not a wise human pursuit. My marriage was slipping away a little at a time without me realizing that there were important parts of life that I wasn't attending to.

Even though I was beginning to be aware of the problems, I did very little to correct them. The excitement of being involved in such a variety of musical areas led me to ignore some basic important parts of life. It is amazing to me that my wife Charlotte did not divorce me much sooner.

A couple of weeks after returning to New York from the *Mass* I was happily engaged to be a part of the revival of another Bernstein show, *On the Town*. This was not only an exciting show to be playing but also a special treat because I was sitting next to one of my all-time heroes Vincent J. (Jimmy) Abato.

Every show was a lesson in musical perfection as I observed Jimmy's gorgeous sound and flawless technique on both the saxophone and clarinet. He was a legendary figure and it was indeed an honor to be making music with him. Being with him for long periods posed a problem as he was an incessant talker. Jimmy Abato was one of New York's more colorful cats who possessed a voluminous vocabulary. He could talk your ear off, for hours at a time, with lengthy stories on a variety of subjects as well as elongated idle chatter.

One prominent New York woodwind player Romeo Penque's description of Jimmy was that "he could turn an empty room into bedlam." I had several experiences with Jimmy where we, unfortunately, bumped heads. He was fun to be around for the most part but had a propensity for stirring things up.

About two months into the run of *On the Town* I did a recording for a new show called *Twigs*. This was not a musical but had an underscore for solo saxophone. The music was a nifty melody written by Stephan Sondheim and played between the three acts of this dramatic comedy. Doing the recording was a notable experience for me. Aside from me and the recording engineer, present in the studio were Stephan Sondheim the producer, Frederic Brisson and his wife the actress Rosalind Russell, and the director Michael Bennett all seated 15 feet directly in front of me while I recorded Mr. Sondheim's charming bitter-sweet melodies.

Since the *Twigs* management insisted on using the recording for the run of the show, a rift ensued with the musician's union. After some tense negotiations, it was ruled that the show could do whatever they chose so long as a payment was made to a live performer for every show. The ruling further stipulated that since I made the recording that I should be hired. If I were to decline the job, they were free to hire whomever they wanted. Since that meant that it would be possible for them to hire anyone including a secretary from their office I was advised to leave *On the Town* and accept the offer.

I was somewhat apprehensive about leaving my job but I was pleasantly surprised when the conductor, Milton Rosenstock offered no resistance to my inquiry. Everything was fine until Mr. Abato got wind of the situation and even though it was no concern of his, decided that I should not be permitted to leave.

Naturally, a major ruckus ensued between me and Mr. Abato. The conductor was convinced by Jimmy and now I had a problem dealing with the two of them since I had already legally started the proceedings with the *Twigs* management. After a couple of screaming arguments with my two antagonists and my threats to demand a union hearing, I was finally permitted to make the change.

Saxophone Troubadour

Needless to say, Jimmy and I went for a few weeks without speaking to each other but fortunately, time healed the wounds, and I was able to stay friends with my idol. I sadly went to his home on Long Island to say goodbye to him when he retired in Florida. He passed away a year later.

The show *Twigs* was a hit and for me, a fabulous deal since my recording was being used. This simply meant that I was doing a Broadway show with all of the benefits attached but was not required to perform live. I did feel a bit like I was featherbedding but an agreement was made and had to be upheld. The slippery slope was that for me to take jobs that conflicted with the *Twigs* schedule an alternate person had to be paid.

I was warned to be particularly careful on this matter; if I were to violate the terms by working another engagement that corresponded with the show schedule I could be dismissed by the company. This created a pleasurable opportunity to dole out sub work to unemployed colleagues. My favorite recipient was Al Cohn, another idol of mine, a leading jazz saxophonist/arranger, who was constantly between engagements. When I phoned him, I would ask, "Al are you working tomorrow night?" When he answered no I would say, "Well don't, stay home so I can send you a check." Al would cheerfully answer "I will put on my *walking** shoes. Al Cohn was a great jazz artist, who was not only considered by many to be an American treasure but an equally comedic personality as well. I consider myself most fortunate to have been in association with such an artist.

*Walking is the musician's term for getting paid per union contract when management decides to employ fewer workers for a given engagement than agreed upon in the working labor agreement. Those who did not actually work but were required to be paid to support the minimum number of players' agreement per theatre were designated as *walkers*.

Musings on a Musical Journey

Twigs was an opportunity to expand musically in that it allowed me to take three weeks off in July to attend the Marlboro Music Festival in beautiful Vermont. It was an amazing treat to be a part of an acclaimed musical retreat that featured top artists from around the world playing the world's greatest music. It was something of a vacation but because of the high abundance of artistry, the pressure to be in top form technically was ever-present. It was a supreme honor to make music with such international artists as Pablo Casals and Rudolf Serkin. My biggest thrill came with having the opportunity to perform the *Mozart piano trio in Eb* with the legendary Austrian pianist Walter Klein.

Twigs closed in 1972 and I again went show hopping, as it were. A pleasant musical entitled *Ambassador* based on Henry James' novel had a short run after being wasted by the cruel New York critics. I thought it was a pretty good show, but what do I know? Following that show, I was involved in the revival of *Pajama Game* which was very enjoyable but short-lived.

There were some notable tunes in that show such as Hernando's *Hideaway*, *Steam Heat,* and my favorite *Hey There*. When it first opened in 1954 it was an immediate success thanks to such Broadway notables as director George Abbott and choreographer Bob Fosse and a wonderful book adaptation by Richard Bissell.

The 1973 revival had a star-studded cast led by Hal Linden, Cab Calloway, and Barbara McNair. Unfortunately, they were not enough to pull the show through one of the worst droughts in Broadway history. Excessive crime, prostitution, and dope peddling in New York led to declining box-office receipts, the largest drop in the entire history of Broadway. The Times Square area of Manhattan was not exactly a welcoming place for the average theatergoer.

Saxophone Troubadour

Movies such as Martin Scorsese's *Taxi Driver* painted an accurate picture of New York City violence in the early 1970s. Even with financial support from several people including Cab Calloway himself, the show sadly closed in February of 1974.

My streak of good fortune continued however with employment in another enjoyable musical *Over Here.* This one opened in March of 1974 and featured Patty Andrews of World War II's famed singing trio the Andrew Sisters. Several newcomers at the time such as Ann Reinking, John Travolta, Treat Williams, and Marilu Henner groomed their talents in the show and went on to successful careers after the closing.

Also featured was a 1940s style big-band arrayed in gold sequined coats seated on stage with a ballroom set. It had a razzmatazz score, razzle-dazzle dancing, and extraordinary choreography by Patricia Birch. The dancers, led mainly by Ann Reinking, were first class. The music was loud and brassy but a good reflection of the early big band era. *Over Here* by all accounts was a hit show but because of a salary dispute between the star Patty Andrews and the show producers, it was abruptly closed. The entire cast was dumbfounded and saddened but such is the way of show biz. Two weeks-notice reared its ugly head once again and the show closed January 4, 1975.

I was again lucky in that I was immediately employed in the civil war musical *Shenandoah*. It fit like a glove, as they say, in that it began on January 7, 1975. I went from being on the stage with a big band at the Shubert Theatre on Shubert Alley to back in the pit at the historic Alvin Theatre on West 52nd Street.

The Alvin Theatre is still my favorite venue in that it has wonderful acoustics. It is now named the Neil Simon Theater in honor of the iconic playwright but to me, it will

Musings on a Musical Journey

always be the Alvin. George Gershwin selected that theater with its perfect sound for the opening of his famous opera *Porgy and Bess*. No amplification was needed because of the wonderful sound ambiance which made it a dream for the singers and instrumentalists.

At one point in *Shenandoah*, I had a distinguishable solo clarinet cadenza which I savored at every performance. The sound could be felt to fill the entire theatre space with a minimum of physical volume exertion and no electronic amplification. On performances when the solo felt really good to me, it was an ego boost to relish the sound that seemed to fill every nook and cranny of that fabulous space.

A notable event in New York City history occurred on July 13, 1977. At approximately 6:45 pm a major black-out took place that threw the city into violent upheaval. I was seated with five of my colleagues enjoying our Saturday poker game which occurred regularly between matinee and evening shows. With no warning, the Majestic Theater, where the show had relocated a year earlier, was thrust into darkness. The theatre was already nearly full of customers waiting to see the 7 pm performance.

To keep the audience safe and avoid a rush to exit the theater, the management decided to proceed with the performance using hand-held flashlights. After a disastrous hour of trying to perform the show in less than tolerable conditions, it was finally decided to abandon the plan and desert the theatre in an orderly manner. The retreat from the theatre was very well managed and the crowd exited from the house without problems.

Unfortunately, New York City was not without incident in that violence including looting, muggings, and arson were rampant. It was not safe to be on the streets that evening. Because there were no subway or bus services in operation, I offered my friend Joe Wilder a ride home. Since

Saxophone Troubadour

I lived in New Jersey and Joe lived on the upper west side at Riverside Drive and West 148th Street I would be passing right by his building.

Joe was a personable happy go lucky trumpet player who was a slight man of not much more than five feet tall. He was a notable figure in American Jazz history who was honored by the prestigious National Endowment for the Arts Award.

An immaculate dresser, Joe was someone who I never saw without a suit, white shirt, and tie. He was one of the most popular musicians in town. I used to call him Mr. Mayor since it would be impossible to walk more than one block on New York streets with him before he would have to stop to talk with one of his many acquaintances. Joe also was a licensed gun owner and an avid photographer who was always in possession of a trusty .45 caliber automatic pistol as well as a highly professionally lensed Leica 35-millimeter camera.

Because no streetlights or traffic lights were working, I decided to drive directly up Broadway to 147th Street. All the way uptown from West 50th Street we passed countless criminal acts, mostly broken storefront windows with many lootings. As I was about to make a left turn on West 147th Street, Joe suddenly got an urge to take some photos of a group looting an electronics store.

Joe hopped out of the car as I waited while he proceeded to get some pictures. He had taken a couple of shots when one of the thugs tore at Joe in an attempt to take the camera away from him. This proved to be not such a good idea for the aggressor when Joe produced his .45 and aimed it point-blank at the man who was no less than ten feet away from him.

I was horror-stricken and thought we were going to have to make a quick getaway from a crime scene.

Musings on a Musical Journey

Fortunately, the bad guy did an abrupt U-turn and beat it back to his mob friends without incident. We proceeded west on 147th Street to Riverside Drive and I deposited Joe at his West 148th Street apartment building. I caught my breath and wiped the sweat from my soaked face, relieved that Joe was packing that gun but even happier that he didn't have to use it. It was one of the scariest experiences in my Gotham years. Bidding Joe adieu I thanked him for keeping his cool and not pulling the trigger.

Between acts on a snowy/icy January night in 1977, I was seated in the *Shenandoah* pit preparing for act II when a familiar face appeared over the pit railing and called out to me. I immediately recognized the face of Dan Patrylak who I knew was an outstanding trumpet player and college educator. We had several mutual acquaintances but had never met. We chatted for a few moments and decided to continue our meeting at a local pub near the theatre after the show.

It turned out that Dan was stranded in New York because of the weather, and I was set to bunk out in my Seventh Avenue studio to avoid the drive back to New Jersey. We had plenty of time to hang out and enjoy too many martinis at a nearby saloon. After a short period of settling in at a very comfortable cocktail lounge and reviewing all of our mutual acquaintances, Dan asked me if I would be interested in joining the faculty at the University of Texas at Austin.

This took me by complete surprise to which I kind of chuckled and told him how honored I was that he asked but no thanks I was doing well in NY. He persisted and after a couple of Martinis convinced me that I should at least come down and do a master class mainly to check the place out and get an expense-paid trip plus a generous fee. Since I never before had been to Texas it sounded like a great offer. What could it hurt? It turned out to be a life-changing event.

After a pleasant couple of hours of light-hearted banter with Dan, I expressed my interest in going to the university to do the class and told him I would think about the job offer. My mind was already made up to be sure. Why on Earth would I ever want to leave New York at this stage of the game to go to Austin, Texas? The following month I found myself on a plane going to Austin with my saxophone and not much master class preparation.

I was thinking this was a foolish lark. It was certainly not something that was going to materialize into anything beyond a couple of days' adventure into the unknown, coupled with some delicious Texas Bar-B-Que. Otherwise, my tongue was in my cheek at the slightest thought of relocating to the Lone-Star State. To my amazement, flying into Austin and witnessing the lush green gorgeous terrain of the Texas hill country from the airplane caught me off guard. This was not the dust bowl I imagined it to be.

Seeing the University of Texas blew me away as well. This unbelievably beautiful campus was much more than I had imagined. The huge architecturally smart Spanish-style buildings proved that nothing is small or understated in Texas. Seeing the infamous University of Texas tower, the scene of the horrific gun massacre in 1966 standing as the centerpiece of this magnificent campus gave me the chills. The pristine landscape enhanced by a plethora of magnolia trees as well as manicured tropical foliage lent an air of a resort. All most impressive and enormously different from New York.

Dan Patrylak gave me an abbreviated but most impressive tour of the campus after which we returned to his studio where we had a nice lunch followed by a brief explanation of how to proceed in the master class. His description was low-key and unlike Texas, it was very understated. He said, "Just tell them about your life in New York, what you do and how you do it" was the gist of his instructions.

When he led me into a large lecture-type classroom, I almost fainted. Expecting to see a few starry-eyed young saxophone students that I could casually converse with, I was shocked to walk in on over 100 eager students. This was a class situation that consisted of all levels of academics from freshmen to graduates. These were serious players of an assortment of woodwinds, from clarinetists, oboists, flutists, and of course saxophonists who were all there to gather information. My unassuming happy-go-lucky attitude suddenly turned into that of a horror-stricken animal caught in a cage with no escape and I pondered "How did I get myself into this?"

After several minutes of mumbling through a personal introduction and the typical conversation to get acquainted, I relaxed and found that I had more to talk about than I first realized. The variety of New York work that I was doing at the time was of interest to the class in that they seemed not to be aware of the various musical possibilities. As my confidence grew, I found that an interest in talking to enthusiastic listeners was going from the terror of a few moments earlier to a feeling of elation at wanting to give them a realistic picture of the working musician's journey in the big city.

In addition to verbally describing my work, I was fortunate to have had my saxophone available to give them an actual example of my playing. Since I had been scheduled to do a saxophone concerto with the prestigious Contemporary Chamber Ensemble of New York the following week, the timing could not have been better. The concerto featured a flurry of a technique-filled cadenza that

Saxophone Troubadour

I had spent the last six months preparing. This was not only an ideal place for a dress rehearsal but a perfectly timed situation in which to show off a modern example of tricky performance techniques. Fortunately, it came off well and the class seemed to be very impressed, as was Dr. Patrylak.

I was really into the experience and after an hour and a half of much banter, mixed with actual playing examples, I was sorry to see the class end. This was followed by a trip to the aforementioned University Tower which housed the officials of the school including the university president.

I was again surprised by Dan when he led me into the office of a high-ranking administrator whose title I never learned. He could have been the president for all I knew. I did assume that he was very important since his office was on the top floor of the tower. It occurred to me that would not have been a good location to have been in when the gunman started his murderous rampage in 1961.

I thought my mind was already made up when I entered the office and felt that, as attractive as this place is, "It ain't The Big Apple". And there was no possibility that I would ever move there. The administrator was behind a pristine-polished magnificent oak desk which held numerous examples of Texas memorabilia as well as an assortment of what appeared to be family pictures. He was comfortably seated in a plush leather desk chair with his gleaming shiny alligator boots cross-legged and thrust upon the end of the desk. I learned that day that in Texas they are not called boots but instead referred to as *shit-kickers.*

He reminded me of a middle-aged Steve McQueen with a slick crew cut. He was jacketless but wore a tight-fitting western-styled dress shirt with a collar that seemed an inch too small, adding a shade of redness to his neck. Could this be where the term redneck came from? It was all finished off with the traditional Texas string tie. He didn't have to speak more than two words before you knew that he was the real McCoy Texan.

After a pleasant meeting, handshake, and the customary acquaintance dialogue I handed him my 10-page resumé. He spent several minutes perusing it carefully and finally looked up remarking, "This is an impressive collection of experiences, why do you want to come to Texas?"

I was again taken by surprise and had no idea of how to answer since I had no intention of becoming a teacher. I was a rank-and-file side man freelancer in New York and my mind was again asking "What are you doing here? You don't want this"

Not knowing how to respond to the Texan's question I only knew that it would not be appropriate to say I did not want the job, but instead I unwittingly blurted out, "Someone once told me, that if you keep moving, they can't hit you."

Out of the corner of my eye I could see Dan Patrylak's face turning to crimson and I'm thinking to myself, *Why did I say that? I never heard that line before.*

After a brief excruciating silence, the administrator burst into a real out-and-out Texas hoot. He was laughing so hard I thought his overtight collar was going to burst. Dan seemingly relaxed and I was surprised and bewildered at the whole situation. The administrator seemed to appreciate my unabashed candor. At that point, I was thinking that I couldn't get out of there fast enough when Dan and the administrator go into a huddle. The next thing I know they're offering me a position as a Visiting Professor, which was a one-year hire with a possibility of an extension.

This was not acceptable under any condition and I'm thinking, great!! This is a graceful way to get off the hook. There was no way that even if I wanted the job, I would

Saxophone Troubadour

transplant to Austin, Texas on speculation. Selling our house in Emerson, New Jersey was not an option. I was sighing a breath of relief that all of this would soon be over. I explained that this would not work as it was too risky a move for me and my family at this stage of the game. Again, another huddle, and after a few minutes, they came back with the offer of an appointment as an Associate Professor with tenure.

This meant that I was to have job security to at least the age of 65. Now I was at the point of just coming out with the truth and admitting that this was all folly when the administrator seemed to sense my hesitation and added a generous salary offer to the pot. At this point, I was totally confused and thinking how ridiculous this was. If I really wanted the job, they probably would not have been interested in hiring me. Go figure???!!!!

The trip back home had me doing a lot of soul-searching as to whether or not this might be a good career move after all. My marriage was deteriorating, and I wondered if this might be a way to get it back on track with a more relaxed lifestyle and a fresh start. Also, part of the agreement was that the university was very much interested in my continuing to work with the New York Philharmonic as a matter of prestige to attract students. Since my work as a saxophonist would generally not exceed 10 weeks during the academic year, they felt it was a workable condition.

In addition, it would be possible to work in New York between May 10th and August 15th during the summer break period. This was all too good to be true and an offer that would be difficult to refuse. In addition to being a prestigious position, it allowed for me to maintain a certain number of New York performing contacts.

Musings on a Musical Journey

By the time I stepped off the plane I was starting to think that moving to Austin, Texas might not be such a bad idea after all. After convincing myself that it might be the thing to do, I approached my wife who was decidedly not in favor of such an upheaval. She was already feeling unsure about our relationship for a variety of justified reasons. The upheaval of a move was certain to be a precursor to the inevitability of a split.

My thinking was that things would improve with a new beginning. I could not have been more wrong. Personally, it was a good move for my career but not my marriage. Everyone I consulted was adamant in advising that I should not make the move. Why leave New York when things were going so well? I was ready to discard this whole idea as an ill-conceived pipedream until I asked the famous flutist Julius Baker for his suggestion. Mr. Baker was not only the principal solo flutist of the New York Philharmonic but to many the best player of that instrument in the world.

Julie, as he was affectionately known, gave me insights that were not only invaluable but turned out to be the advice that decided my fate. His suggestions were unique and opposite to any others I received. "Make the change," he said immediately, looking me straight in the eye. "You'll come back better than ever." were his words that I will always remember. Julie continued, "I've been changing all of my life and every step was up."

He was a very wise experienced individual, and I am forever grateful for his foresight and thoughtfully honest advice. Now I was certain, and nothing was going to stop me from convincing my wife that we should make this move. When she realized my intentions, she was devastated and quite depressed for some time. I did feel that in time she would come around, which she did in a way, after performance and teaching opportunities came her way not long after we settled in.

Except for family problems that manifested themselves from day one in Texas, I loved the job, the university, Austin, and most of all the barbeque. Even though there were a few peaceful interludes, the marriage spiraled downward steadily. I was able to manage a saxophone studio of 18 students, with the aid of an assistant, and still keep physical contact with work in New York City.

Summer-time breaks turned out to be wonderful in that we were able to house-sit for Paige and Alice Brook in Dumont, New Jersey. The Brooks would spend the summers in Maine at their other home and they were as delighted as we were that we could keep the home fires burning. It was a spectacular arrangement for us both. Paige was the associate principal flutist of the New York Philharmonic and Alice was recently retired as Leonard Bernstein's personal secretary.

The best perk with this arrangement was that I was able to keep Broadway on my schedule. A contractor, Earl Shendell that I had worked for previously was happy when I was available and always came up with work for me. Between the years 1977 and 1980 he was able to hire me to start four different shows. They were *Angel* (1978), a musical adaptation based on Thomas Wolfe's *Look Homeward Angel; Blackstone* (1978) magic show; a revival of Sammy Davis' *Golden Boy* in 1979; and *Peter Pan* also in 1979. Except for *Angel* all were relative hits so I was living the best of both work worlds.

As for my marriage, things were getting away from us a little more each day. Even with a few happy moments during the Texas years, the die was cast. It was apparent that our marriage was not going to continue much longer. It was a hard-to-take realization after having been together

Musings on a Musical Journey

for 24 years, married for 22, and with a very beautiful and talented daughter, Marissa.

After three academic years in Texas, it was not difficult to resign my position and head back to New York. This was the late 1970s when the cost of living had risen to a rate of 16%, so life in Austin was not as comfortable financially as it had been three years earlier. The average rate of pay raises in the Texas university system was 5% per year. If things continued along those lines the financial part of this engagement was not going to be lucrative in a few short years.

I was hoping against hope that a move back to the Apple would magically bring us back together. When the dean of the school of arts called me in to ask my reasons for leaving such a great job I simply said, "I really do not want to leave, I would like a 15-year sabbatical." I supposed that as long as I came in with a smart-ass statement I might as well go out with one. It was truthful in that I felt the need to get the performing aspect of my life out of the way to become a mature teacher. I did not feel the need to relate to him the problems of my personal life nor the fact that salary issues were considerations.

We made the break in July of 1980 and went back to the New York Metropolitan area. After buying a house in Ridgewood, New Jersey we attempted to get a fresh start, but it turned into the beginning of 10 of the unhappiest years of my life. We had not been back for more than a month when I received an invitation to go on a five-week tour of Greece with the American Symphony Orchestra. It was a terrific engagement in several ways, key among those was the prospect of a great way to see exotic places in a far-away country that I would never have been likely to see otherwise.

Saxophone Troubadour

Although it was a rather long time to be away, it seemed at the time to be a good way to be alone with my thoughts. It was a wonderful musical experience as well as I could get my playing back to the necessary level of full-time, top of my game, NYC day to day work schedules. The tour turned out to be all that I hoped for and more.

Returning home, however, brought a not totally unexpected, unpleasant surprise. My wife told me she wanted a separation, and it became apparent that our marriage was about to end. Even though I knew we were not destined to continue, it was hard for me to comprehend that an actual divorce was now on the horizon. Marriage counseling only seemed to escalate the problems and a final divorce was set into motion.

Fortunately, I was employed again shortly after arriving back home and spent the better part of each day trying to comprehend all that was happening, how to proceed with life for my daughter, as well as for myself, and working on Broadway. The show I was called to do was based on Lerner and Loewe's 1954 film *Brigadoon*. The revival was recreated as a Broadway musical and opened on October 16, 1980, at the Majestic Theatre with fabulous choreography by Agnes DeMille and the wonderful and quirky musical director Wally Harper.

Thankfully the show was a fine experience both musically and personally. The stress of my home situation was lightened by the workplace experience of musical associations that were exemplary. The legendary bassoonist Sandy Sharoff was in the woodwind section which was particularly great personally in that I would often get to play chamber music with him before and after performances. In addition, we would frequently be joined by my daughter Marissa, who at age 12 was already a fine violinist able to more than hold her own in mature music-making. Even

Musings on a Musical Journey

though *Brigadoon* had a relatively short five-month run from October 16, 1980, to February 8, 1981, it couldn't have come at a better time in that it softened the blow of all that was transpiring at home.

Getting re-settled back home in Ridgewood, New Jersey was, to say the least, unsettling but being hired to do a show called *El Bravo* took the edge off. The show turned out a be a complete bomb according to the NY Times, but from where I sat it was quite enjoyable. It was staged at the Entermedia Theatre which was located on the corner of East 12th Street and Second Avenue, quite a distance from Broadway but right in the middle of some of the finest dining areas of the city.

The Second Avenue Deli was just up the street and one block over on First Avenue was the Polish restaurant section which was as authentic as anything in Warsaw. I enjoyed the area as well as the show. *El Bravo* was directed by Louis St. Louis, famously known for being the brains behind the mega-hit *Grease*. Again, I was surrounded by a overabundance of talent but unfortunately, the show only ran for 48 performances and closed on June 17, 1981.

Fate came through with a schedule that seemed perfectly timed to get things on the right track. A phone call from Bill LaVorgna, Liza Minnelli's conductor and drummer was an inquiry about a recommendation for a sax player to go on a four-month tour of the United States, Hawaii, Australia, China, Japan, and the Philippines. Without giving it much thought, I immediately said, "Yes I would like to recommend myself."

Under ordinary circumstances, a trip such as that would have been out of the question. To leave the city for such a prolonged period would not be a good business move but under the prevailing conditions, it was perfectly timed to give my wife four months to make up her mind about

Saxophone Troubadour

what she wanted and to move on if that was what she decided.

The tour was a mixture of a wonderful exotic adventure coupled with depression I had never known. The Liza gig itself is a subject for another chapter but suffice to say it served its purpose and the divorce was now all but settled. After four months on the road, it was now time to get back to New York to put my personal life back together as well as my life as a New York freelancer.

I had just returned home from the four-month Liza tour and was immediately hooked up to do the show *Cats* which was set to open at the Winter Garden Theatre in 1982. Ben Aronov, pianist and Ross Konikoff, trumpet, and I were all recruited from Liza's band to join the opening. It was an honor to be with players such as Ben, Ross, the Panamanian trumpet virtuoso Victor Paz and a fine orchestra. *Cats* proved to be a great benefit personally, in that it made six years of my daughter's college bill financially viable.

While playing *Cats* at the Winter Garden I learned some interesting facts about the history of the theatre. It was built in 1896 by William Vanderbilt and designed to house New York City's carriage trade. Because it stabled horses, a large round opening was constructed at the apex of the building to air out the obnoxious scents that emanated from within. When the automobile industry took over the country, Warner Brothers bought the building and made it into a movie theatre. The reconstruction consisted of installing a swimming pool to allow for several of Esther Williams' movies to be filmed. Eventually the swimming pool was redesigned into an orchestra locker room/ lounge after the Shubert Company turned the Winter Garden into one of Broadway's premiere houses.

Musings on a Musical Journey

With Broadway's surge in the early 1900s, the theatre was given a glitzy makeover that featured luxurious gold-leaf throughout the interior. The golden ceiling and fixtures remained for 70 odd years. Then the musical *Cats* came along and required the entire interior to become a setting of a junkyard to fill the needs of the production.

As a result, it took extra time to prepare the building, especially to remove the gold interior. In 1981, the estimated cost of the razing alone was over $1,000,000. The biggest surprise came when six inches of mold was found under the gold leaf. This was the result of years of horse manure and swimming pool humidity. I now understood the distinct aroma that permeated the hall at all times. I actually liked the smell as it gave me a feeling of really being a part of the theatre world. Could this possibly be the reason for my feeble brain?

Situated on the corner of 50th Street and Broadway was Hawaii Kai, a popular tourist nightclub/ restaurant. It was housed in a lush three-story structure that was attached to the Winter Garden and attracted stars as well as tourists. Part of the attraction was the many pictures on the walls of scenes from Hollywood films, most notably *Goodfellows*. A fire in the early 1980s as well as declining popularity forced the closure of the restaurant in 1989.

The effects of the closing were felt at the Winter Garden when the building was partly razed and redesigned. Large NYC rats took up residence in the bowels of the theatre, mainly in the basement quarters of the musicians' locker room as well as the walls throughout. One fateful night, I noticed a large creature roaming along the edge of a row of storage lockers. I thought, "Why do people bring their pet dogs down here?" My disgust turned to horror when I realized this was not a cocker spaniel, but a full-sized rodent of similar proportions. Yuck!

Saxophone Troubadour

Cats, however, was a dream job in many ways including that it made it possible for me to be part of Garrison Keillor's *American Radio Show*, formerly *Prairie Home Companion* orchestra.

The radio show worked on Fridays and Saturdays, so it was possible to sandwich that gig in since we were permitted to work outside engagements up to 50% of the workweek as per union rules. Garrison Keeler's show was a delight to do in every way. It was one of the happiest collaborations that I was ever a part of for six years of my career. It was a live show and the closest I came to fulfilling my original dream of playing on a radio show broadcasting live from New York. Everything about that experience was first class.

Speaking of good fortune, I was ecstatic to meet the love of my life in 1990. Rosalie Jackson became Rosy Regni in 1992. After living 10 years with a mixture of joy, frustration, and depression, I now found myself in Utopia. Rosy was and remains more than I could ever have hoped for. She has been the glue in our family and my daughter Marissa's beloved wicked stepmother. The period of 10 years between my divorce and waiting to find Rosy turned out to be the wisest choice I made in my life.

In the year following our marriage, I came to realize that I could now manage to leave the security of *Cats* and branch out with a new adventure. *Cats* was a dream show in many ways but after 10 years I now had the opportunity to search out a new adventure. The chance to start a Broadway show entitled *The Goodbye Girl* was appealing as one of my all-time favorite musical arrangers, Billy Byers was doing the show. Rosy and I took a trip to Chicago for an out-of-town preview to see if the show appealed.

Musings on a Musical Journey

With a book by Neil Simon, music by Marvin Hamlisch, performers Bernadette Peters and Martin Short in addition to Billy Byers, I decided it was well worth the gamble.

Additionally, I reasoned that after 30 years of doing Broadway it was time to stretch out and take on some new musical adventures. Doing the show was a treat in many ways but unfortunately, *The Goodbye Girl* said goodbye to Broadway and closed on August 15, 1993, after a disappointing six-month run.

I was very fortunate to have been introduced to the well-known composer/arranger/orchestrator Jonathan Tunick when we were students at the Eastman School of Music some 35 years earlier. I worked for Jonathan many times on Broadway shows as well as recordings and live venues. Although I did not do as many of his shows as I would have liked because of other commitments, he continued to call with offers.

When *The Good-Bye Girl* closed, he immediately called to see if I might be interested in working on an off-Broadway production of *The Petrified Prince*. It was an interesting show that was to open at the Public Theatre in lower Manhattan. It was an artsy type of musical that was not the usual big Broadway production, but rather, an intimate one. Quite a change from the big brassy shows I had been accustomed to for so many years.

In the beautiful setting of the limited seating Public Theatre, it was a pleasure to be a part of a more delicate endeavor. The trip to the lower East Side of Manhattan for eight shows a week became a chore after a while and I was pleased when Jonathan offered me a chair in Stephen Sondheim's new musical *Passion* which was set to open in the heart of Broadway at the Plymouth Theatre.

For me, *Passion* was among the best of Sondheim's works. It bordered on serious opera and was a very low-

Saxophone Troubadour

keyed, quiet musical that required a classical interpretation approach.

Unlike the usual Broadway musical, there were no references to jazz renderings in this show. In many ways, it required a chamber music sensitivity that kept us carefully listening to the stage singers and underscore as well as to each other. In short, it was a wonderful experience from a musician's point of view.

After doing *Passion* for approximately six months, I was offered an opportunity to leave to do the big musical *Victor, Victoria* starring Julie Andrews.

This offer was hard to turn down because it again had Billy Byers as arranger/orchestrator doing the music of the famous Henry Mancini. The star power of Julie Andrews pulled the show through some less than rave reviews and it was deemed a hit. As we all expected Ms. Andrews was everything that we hoped for, and the show turned out to be a good experience.

It was exciting to hear Julie pop off the extremely high, virtuoso soprano parts that were required of her, until the rigors of eight shows a week took their toll on her singing apparatus. She was encouraged to endure unnecessary serious vocal surgery which regretfully led to her eventual retirement from the show.

Since *Victor, Victoria* appeared to be winding down when Julie Andrews was being replaced, I decided the offer to do a new show entitled *Big* was worthy of serious consideration. This was a Broadway rendering of the well-known Tom Hanks movie several years earlier. I left *Victor, Victoria* in 1996 and was excited to be part of David Shire and Richard Maltby's new work.

Many felt the show was a good one, but the New York critics did not agree and as far as I was concerned did a hack job, as they say. *Big* did not get the run-on Broadway that it deserved, but such is the way of the cruel critics on show business.

It had been re-written later, and the national road production was a hit. Alas, the Broadway production closed after six months and 193 performances.

Jonathan Tunick came to the rescue once again by hiring me to do a neat new musical starring Treat Williams called *Captains Courageous* which started at the Manhattan Theatre Club on January 12, 1999. The show was based on the 1897 novel by Rudyard Kipling and written by the team of Frederic Fryer, (music), and Patrick Cook (lyrics and book). Jonathan's orchestrating was typical of his first-class work and a joy to be part of. Even though *Captains Courageous* had a limited four-month run it was a pleasurable engagement in the comfortable setting of New York's Center Stage which was located in the City Center of New York on West 55th Street.

The closing of *Captains Courageous* was the precursor to my desire to finish off a Broadway career, as I began thinking of a new beginning. After a few months of doing substitute work, I was offered the show *Titanic* by Jonathan Tunick and decided that eight shows a week was not what I should be doing after 38 years of going in and out of every stage door in New York.

I turned the show down thinking that a sub gig now and then would be enough. I found myself subbing in the hit show *The Producers* on a Sunday matinee and thinking of my bride sitting home. It was now time to take the next step and pull the plug on an excitingly wonderful, if sometimes tedious part of my life. It came to me as if I were snapping a light switch. The bright lights of Broadway were now dark in my mind, and I did my last show in the pit of New York's St. James Theatre on a Sunday Matinee, February 10, 2002.

Chapter 6
Recordings, TV, Movies, Studio Work, and Teaching, 1960-2000

Sometimes, juggling work became a problem because I only knew how to say *yes*. The variety of work that I encountered during the years 1960 to 2000 kept me busy even though each area could be sporadic. For example, concerts, recordings, movies, TV, and various studio gigs were subject to ups and downs in availability. My preference was to maintain as many potential areas as possible to keep a variety of involvement in the event of drought periods in each field.

I did maintain my number one preference, the New York Philharmonic. I felt it was an area where my employment would not fluctuate. And I could expect to have anywhere from five to 20 weeks a year as a good extension of my theater and commercial work. This occasionally posed a problem in deciding which to accommodate in maintaining a foothold in all areas.

Studio Work and Recording Dates

The most lucrative and most highly competitive work was in the studios. Studio work was also subject to hot and cold periods, so getting an opportunity to become active in this sector could be tricky.

Musings on a Musical Journey

My first chance at doing a top New York recording engagement was as a replacement for the legendary Al Gallodoro. Al was considered to be the top woodwind New York doubler of his day. I was called in because a major snowstorm in January 1963 crippled New York City. Other players either were unable to get to the studio or did not want to risk traveling in 20 inches of snow. I probably was the 30th person that contractor Carl Prager called to play clarinet on a TV commercial written by the legendary Sid Ramin.

Because it was a TV commitment, the session could not be postponed and therefore had to be done regardless of the weather. Being the young over-zealous new kid on the block I decided there was nothing that was going to stop me from getting to the session.

Sid Ramin was best known for his arranging work on West Side Story as well as numerous TV, motion pictures, and commercial recordings. He was certainly a musical luminary and among the best of the best. When I learned that it was his session, I decided turning him down was not an option.

Since all public transportation was suspended, the only way to get to A & R recording studios on West 48th Street was on foot. And the only way to trek on foot was to walk straight down the center of Broadway since that was the only plowed surface available. With 20 inches of snow on the ground, there was virtually no traffic.

My apartment at that time was at 535 West 110th Street, 62 blocks north of A & R Studios. NY City estimates of 20 blocks per mile meant it was a little over three miles. I wonder if getting to a recording session, under those circumstances, could have made it into the Guinness Book of World Records? The things one has to do to stay in show biz, as they say.

Saxophone Troubadour

Arriving at that date and having a successful performance for Sid Ramin paid dividends, as I was hired by him for many recordings over the following 20 years.

The 1960s through the 1980s was a significant period for recordings and concerts of American contemporary music, much of it done by Nonesuch Records and various new ensembles. The record company was headed by the impresario Ms. Tracy Stern.

Groups that did much of the work both on recordings and in concert halls were The Contemporary Ensemble, The Group for Contemporary Music, Da Capo, Speculum Musicae, and the New York New Music Ensemble.

In addition, there were various concert series, most notably the Rug concerts and Prospective Encounters under the auspices of the New York Philharmonic. These were special as they were conducted by Pierre Boulez who we all thought had such sensitive ears that he could hear paint drying. It was very necessary to know one's part thoroughly when you played under him.

Since saxophone parts were relatively rare, I was fortunate to have been on the roster to play with these groups. And during that time, I performed on several recordings and live performances. It was an exciting period for me because the performance standards were very high, and it was certainly a pleasure to work with the extraordinary musicians involved. Jan DeGaetani, Gilbert Kalish, Paul Dunkel, Jean Ingraham, and Arthur Bloom were a few of the artists who were the standard-bearers of the New York new music scene at the time.

It took extra effort to be a part of these events because of the logistics of pulling all the individual players' schedules together. Rehearsals and recording sessions of classical contemporary music were frequently done late at night, either in someone's apartment or in a remote area of

Musings on a Musical Journey

Manhattan or Brooklyn. More often, the working conditions were less than desirable.

A recording session that comes to mind occurred with the Contemporary Chamber Ensemble directed by Arthur Weisberg. It was *Suite from The Three Penny Opera*, by Kurt Weill and *Creation Du Monde* by Darius Milhaud. These were pieces that both had extensive saxophone parts and they were most exciting for me to be a part of. Mr. Weisberg, a pleasant yet extremely quiet individual was one of the top New York conductors and bassoonists. He managed to keep matters comfortable even under less than desirable working conditions.

An unexpected challenge at these recording sessions, however, was that they were done in the middle of two cold December nights in a dark church on West 73th Street in Manhattan. The location was a wonderful acoustical space but lacked the niceties of a warm well-lit recording studio. Since there were no individual music-stand lights we had to make do with an assortment of floor lamps placed at various intervals within the group. How these recordings came out as well as they did is a testament to the dedicated artists making the music.

I was honored to play on many live concerts and recordings that were nothing less than thrilling. Probably the best of all was the TV documentary recording sessions of Leonard Bernstein's *West Side Story* done in 1984 at RCA studios on West 44th Street in New York City.

With Leonard Bernstein conducting, the cast and orchestra were in ecstasy for the inspiring two weeks it took to complete the project. I believe that Lenny was truly at his best. The completed product is one of the masterpieces in the history of recorded sound. It was the only time in his life that Lenny conducted the work and his enthusiasm spilled over to everyone in that famous studio.

Saxophone Troubadour

Maestro Bernstein made his initial appearance at the first session with his trademark cigarette dangling out of the side of his mouth. He was quick to announce that he was excited to be conducting this for the first time in his life. With the exuberance of a cheerleader, he introduced the leading singers Kiri Te Kanawa and José Carreras with all of the hoopla of a collegiate football game.

Again, the Bernstein magic transformed the room into an environment of relaxed but dynamic creativity. If there was tension it was quickly melted away in his ability to convert the singers, players, and the recording people into a unified ensemble. His manner of patient insistence for what he wanted was a rare trait resulting in the very best from his performers.

It has been a point of contention that the singers Bernstein chose were too operatic in style and not appropriate for the roles. The leading vocalists consisting of Dame Kiri Te Kanawa, José Carreras, Tatiana Troyanos, and Kurt Ollmann were spectacular and, in my opinion, proved the critics' contentions incorrect. I am unable to hear these incredible performances to this day without shedding a tear. José's singing of *Maria,* Dame Kiri's and Mr. Carreras's duet on *One Hand One Heart,* Ms. Troyanos' rendition of *America* are all examples of American music composition and performances at their pinnacle.

Sitting in a reed section consisting of Julius Baker, Andy Lolya, Harvey Estrin, Ron Roseman, Don MacCourt, George Marge, Les Scott, John Campo, Seymour Press, Dave Tofani, and Wally Kane was an honor that I will forever cherish. By any reasonable thought, we all should have been terrified at being in the presence of the great Bernstein, but we were relaxed, and the entire orchestra came through with aplomb. For me, these sessions were nothing short of pure musical euphoria.

Musings on a Musical Journey

Playing on studio recording dates was pretty much a daily occurrence for me during the 1970s and 1980s but it began to dwindle in the 1990s. Technology began to shed new light on the music business, especially in the commercial world of TV and radio advertising. That exciting, fun, and lucrative part of the music scene changed as did endeavors affected by a new era.

Some amusing incidents occurred that are remembered fondly. A concert in 1993 with a new music ensemble at the film theatre of Lincoln Center is a case in point. The soprano Janet Bookspan was soloist in William Walton's *Façade*, a piece for reciter/vocalist and small instrumental ensemble. Madame Bookspan was the wife of Martin Bookspan the radio announcer for the New York Philharmonic. Although she was primarily an opera singer, she was well suited for this work having the exact vocal techniques necessary for the difficult articulations involved.

Since the group was newly formed, we were given complimentary tickets in an attempt to fill the hall and to entice possible subscribers. I had my wife Rosy come to the performance to assist in the reception that was planned after the concert, as well as to hear the music and occupy a seat.

The comp ticket that I was given had seat number A6 which was first-row center. In this smallish theatre, it meant she would be approximately twenty feet from Ms. Bookspan and well within eyesight.

Rosy's propensity for falling asleep in concerts had me a little worried when I noticed she was not only the sole person in the front row but there was no one else seated in the entire first two rows. *Uh oh*, I thought, this can't be good and sure enough Rosy was in the arms of Morpheus about 15 minutes after the start of the program. She was not an inconspicuous sleeper, and it was obvious that those of us

Saxophone Troubadour

on stage were always the most aware of her state of unconsciousness.

I thought I could see steam emanating from Janet Bookspan's nostrils as it was quite apparent that she was not pleased. Rosy on the other hand had a look of complete relaxation and it was apparent that the music was having a distinctly soothing effect on her body's bobbing head.

We of the ensemble had difficulty keeping from breaking out into hilarity but managed to keep our cool. The performance went well even with an occasional inaudible grunt of rage from the soloist's displeasure.

When we were backstage and the applause had ended, Madame Bookspan expressed her displeasure and asked, "O.K., who was that uncouth character in the front row?" She had deduced that Rosy belonged to one of us and was ready to throw a tantrum. Of course, none of us would confess, least of all me.

The diva was all but cooled off until she made her grand entrance into the reception hall. When she laid eyes on Rosy the darts were streaming from her eyes. Before she could start a tirade Rosy offered her a section of the creamy dessert she had made. I wondered if what was called *Cousin Lucy's Dessert* would end up in Rosy's face. Much to my surprise Janet gracefully accepted and immediately took to devouring it. She hadn't taken two bites before a satisfied smile came over her and she suddenly was congratulating Rosy on her wonderful gourmet creation. The smiles turned to frivolity and Rosy was forgiven by all, especially Janet Bookspan.

Movies

Movie work was fun but very challenging to do. Because of tight time constraints and high costs involved in producing movies it was important to play with high degrees of accuracy, as well as to play in the style that the story called for. Over my years of working in New York City, I was able to play in over forty movies.

Among my favorites were *Home Alone II, House Sitters, Fire Walk with Me, Femme Fatale, Get on the Bus, Crooklyn, My Blue Heaven, Power, Cape Fear,* and *Mad Dog and Glory.* Working for the likes of director Spike Lee and composers Elmer Bernstein and Terence Blanchard were highlights of my time in playing on movie scores.

Teaching

I've heard it said that there are no good teachers, only good students. I'm not sure that I agree with that, because I did have some very good instructors. As a teacher, I was fortunate to have had students that taught me as much or more than I taught them.

Except for the three years that I was engaged at The University of Texas as a tenured saxophone professor, my preoccupation and focus had always been on personal performing. Even though I consistently maintained a studio in New York City, teaching was something I would fit in between a schedule of live gigs.

Between the years 1963 and 1973, my teaching was done in the dining room of our apartment on 535 West 110th Street This was a great older building in the Columbia University area of the city. It was just a couple of buildings west of where George Gershwin once lived and composed. There were many musicians in the building so playing instruments was tolerated as long it was between the hours of 9 am and 9 pm. Being a pre-war building it was well constructed with sound-resistant thick walls.

Saxophone Troubadour

I had three different studio locations in the city over the years. The first between 1965 and 1975 was at a very run-down building at 50th Street and 7th Avenue. It had been a studio location for many musicians over the years but by the time I set up there it had seen better days and many of the well-known tenants had moved out. It was a good location in the center of the West Side downtown, but during that period there were many break-ins due to a period of high crime in the city and lack of building security.

I had several bad experiences and after having instruments stolen from the space could never hope to leave anything of value there. I was sorry to leave that studio because immediately across the hall was the great jazz pianist Tony Aless. It was a joy to eavesdrop on the fabulous sounds that filled the hall as well as to converse with him on various musical topics. The stories of his luminous career, especially of having worked with Charlie Parker, were mesmerizing.

In 1977 my career took a somewhat unusual turn when I accepted a full-time position at the University of Texas as associate professor of Saxophone. It took some mental adjusting to realize that I was now first an educator, secondly a performer. Up to that point, my concept was as a performer. I was not fully prepared to assume the role of saxophone pedagogue.

In the six months before assuming that position I went to the legendary Joseph Allard for a course in teaching methods and repertoire. It turned out to be a life-changing experience as I was not only learning the ways of academia but responsible for personal classical solo performing. While my experience and knowledge of classical symphonic music were advanced, I had never performed as a solo recitalist. Mr. Allard not only gave me exposure to the basic materials but worked on my classical performance techniques. This was invaluable for the career course that I was about to begin.

Not all teaching experiences were good, some even terrifying. During a period in the 1980s, I was teaching at the apartment of Dorothy Strahl on Manhattan's Upper West Side. One particular college I was teaching for was Kingsborough Community College of Brooklyn, NY. The school would assign me six to ten students each semester to teach saxophone. It was a particularly good set-up in that the students would come to my location so that I would not have to travel to the outer regions of Brooklyn.

The course of study was co-sponsored by Local 802 Musician's Union, Kingsborough College, and Nassau Community College to assist in training prospective music educators to obtain their New York State teaching credentials.

It was conceived as a very good plan but unfortunately was taken advantage of by some of the students. A few applicants would take the course as a means of getting free lessons or simply to get an easily attainable degree. One such student was Colin Ferguson, better known as the Long Island Railroad shooter.

When Mr. Ferguson first appeared in 1988, I was taken with his neatly dressed appearance. Attired in a well-tailored sport coat, white shirt, tie, topped off with an elegant porkpie hat, it was easy to be impressed by his smart appearance.

Mr. Ferguson was not in the room more than five minutes when he proclaimed that he was a professional saxophonist who had extensive experience in his native country of Jamaica.

His initial comment was "Professor, so as not to waste your time or mine why not just give me an A and I will agree that our course was sufficiently completed?" to which I

Saxophone Troubadour

replied, "You know that we will both get into much trouble if we do that." and I steadfastly refused.

When I was finally able to get him to display his saxophone abilities it became readily apparent that he was a rank beginner. When he became confrontational, it was obvious that this man was delusional and perhaps even dangerous. It didn't take much thought to realize that he needed to be dismissed. We agreed that I would give him an assignment which he would complete at the following week's lesson. If he performed to my satisfaction, I would give him a completed grade of B+. Although he adamantly demanded that the grade be an A, he finally agreed. This was an illegal deed on my part but a step that I deemed necessary.

On December 7, 1993, Colin Ferguson boarded a westbound Long Island Railroad train and brutally murdered six people and wounded nineteen with a semi-automatic handgun. His stated motive was that, during his life, he had been treated unfairly. . . whew!

In 1985 I was able to team up with a voice teacher and two ladies who ran an acting agency for youngsters. We shared the rent on a space at 850 Seventh Ave which was between 54th and 55th Street, another great location, just steps from Carnegie Hall. Agreed upon times that the room would be available to me were evenings after 6 pm and weekends. The building was well maintained, and the spacious studio was on the second floor just above the Carnegie Deli.

On one memorable night, I was looking down from our window immediately over the filming of *Broadway Danny Rose*, a Woody Allen movie. The only problem with that location was that I couldn't stay away from the Carnegie Deli and the overstuffed deli sandwiches. How I miss that chopped liver!

Musings on a Musical Journey

I often taught as many as ten students a week there; usually before, between, and sometimes even after my Broadway show schedule. It was a dream location until the management decided to triple the rent and forced many of the entertainment-related people out of the building in 1990. Typical NY City building realtor's tactics. It frequently struck me as odd that the district surrounding the Broadway theaters was an area where the majority of real estate people did not seem to care about the show business community. I was always saddened when I passed that spot and looked up to see a Chinese restaurant where our studio once was.

A stroke of luck came my way accidentally when I casually asked Andy Lolya, the solo flutist of the New York City Ballet Orchestra if he might know of any available teaching spaces. He was quick to invite me to share his space on the eighth floor of Carnegie Hall since he was nearing retirement and cutting back on his teaching schedule. This was a real treat because the rent was very low since it was under New York City rent control laws.

Being an elite location also made it a drawing card for securing students. Unfortunately, it all came to an end upon the death of Mr. Lolya forcing me to move out because Andy was the owner of the lease. The building management was eager to end their commitment to the rent control law arrangements and therefore refused to extend the rental agreement.

Along with free-lance teaching, I was also employed by many colleges in the NY area over the years. Among them were Lehman College, Brooklyn College, Kings College, Bard College, NY University, Trenton (New Jersey) State College, SUNY Purchase, and Kingsborough College. In addition, I taught for three years as a full-time tenured saxophone professor at the University of Texas at Austin,

Saxophone Troubadour

Texas. Additionally, there were two-semester stints as a sabbatical replacement for Professor Ramon Ricker at the Eastman School of Music in Rochester, New York.

Teaching started as a supplemental way of making ends meet but turned into a good experience that was more than a sideline. Most of the students I worked with were college level but many were of professional status and a pleasure to work with.

Students such as Ray Ricker, David Riekenberg, Rob Lockhart, David Demsey, Paul Ostermayer, James Warth, Donald Harrison, Kenny Garret, Lino Gomez, Charles Pillow, Phil Thompson, Chris Vadala, Michael Chamberlin, and Dan Goble are just some of the instrumentalists I have had the honor to work with and am happy to have seen move on to prosperous careers.

In the 60 years that I spent involved with a variety of student levels, I can safely estimate that there have been over a thousand woodwind players that I had the honor to have tutored.

Musings on a Musical Journey

Chapter 7
Three Memorable Conductors

Having had the opportunity of working with a number and variety of conductors from different styles of music, there were many who left an indelible impression on my memory. Some impressions were less wonderful than others.

A conductor's role traditionally is to understand, interpret and convey the composer's musical intent to a group of players so that it can be listened to intelligently by an audience. Hence, the conductor's job is to tie-in the three essentials of music; composition – performer – listener. Each part is an equal ingredient to the complete musical experience.

Although he was not really a conductor, or for that matter could not even read music, Danny Kaye possessed many of the attributes of a great conductor. Because of his background as a comedian, singer and dancer his ability to give clear and accurate direction was uncanny. He not only had a conception of what the music should sound like, but he could communicate his ideas clearly to the players.

There have been many conductors who were indeed an honor to have played under but three that stand out over 50 years are the following:

Saxophone Troubadour

Leonard Bernstein

It was the fall of 1968, my first time playing for the legend, and I didn't know what to expect. We were all waiting for the rehearsal to begin on the stage of Avery Fisher Hall, also known as Philharmonic Hall at Lincoln Center since its opening in 1962. The hall was renovated in 2015 and renamed David Geffen Hall. The concert hall is the home of the New York Philharmonic and stands as the symphony space at Lincoln Center. The other two main halls, The New York State Theatre (home of the New York City Ballet) and The Metropolitan Opera House are joined by several smaller theatres that house a variety of arts venues that comprise the center.

I had played at Philharmonic Hall on several occasions previously but walking onto the stage on this occasion stands out in my mind because now I would be part of the New York Philharmonic that would be conducted by America's legendary maestro. Seeing this magnificent space with the present expectations was indeed a treasured moment in my life. Even though Philharmonic Hall never surpassed Carnegie Hall as New York's Symphonic mecca it was the newest symbol of the highest artistic musical achievements, and the initial thrill of that personal recollection remains firm.

Seeing the great Leonard Bernstein up close for the first time was indeed an eye-opener. As if on cue, onto the stage popped this human dynamo, still spewing smoke from a recently doused cigarette. He wore the signature suave, mischievous Bernstein smile that puzzled me then, but that I would later come to fondly anticipate. With a dramatic entry, he patted one violinist on the back while shaking hands with another, at the same time bantering typical New York wise-cracks all the way to the podium. I vividly

Musings on a Musical Journey

remember thinking, *Here comes P.T. Barnum, Gustave Mahler, Fiorello LaGuardia, and George Gershwin all wrapped up into one constantly animated man.* What I didn't know at the time was how quickly he would become my forever favorite conductor.

Lenny had a knack for knowing just how to make an entrance whether it be onto a stage or any other space. His simple gesture gave the receiver the impression that he was directing himself solely to him or her.

For me, it was a warm smile, a wave, and a look of familiarity that gave me the feeling that he knew as much about me as I knew about him. I believe that an essential part of this magic was his quality of personal acquaintanceship to whomever he was communicating, whether it be verbal or musical.

Oh sure, he could be totally pompous at times and downright humble at others—a real enigma. It was the extremes of his nature that gave him this unique aura and contributed to the wonder of Leonard Bernstein. One moment he could uplift you with his marvelous musical abilities; another moment he would infuriate you with incredible chutzpah that could border on downright arrogance.

Though I certainly knew he was a master of his many assorted skills, it was amazing to witness his artistry as a conductor, pianist, composer, and educator. He was the personification of a true renaissance man. His piano prowess was among the best of the best and when he dazzled it was with an imposing spirit coupled with an extraordinary technique that was pure ecstasy to the ear.

Add to this his ability to shock with an unusual twist either spoken or musical and he was never boring. As a conductor, Leonard Bernstein's presence was always felt and always electrifying. His conducting movements could

Saxophone Troubadour

sometimes be defined as over-the-top but always inspiring. The educational qualities that he possessed are well documented in the *New York Philharmonic TV Young Peoples' Concerts* as well as his legendary Harvard Lectures which he presented over many years.

At our first meeting, I was still relatively new to the New York Philharmonic, having played with them off and on for the previous three years. I was never a regular member of the orchestra but was called upon regularly to play saxophone when the repertoire called for it. On separate occasions, either as a substitute and/or as an extra, I would be called to play an assortment of clarinets (i.e., e-flat clarinet or bass clarinet) which I eagerly welcomed. My major instrument during my conservatory years was clarinet, so I was comfortably familiar with much of that repertoire.

Most of the pieces that I had played up to that point, however, were directed by guest conductors, since the permanent conductor was only contracted for about 12 weeks of the 40-week season. I realized later that this experience was good for me, as it allowed me to get accustomed to playing with the wonderful players in the New York Phil, like John Corigliano, concertmaster; Saul Goodman, tympanist; Harold Gomberg, principal oboe; Julius Baker, principal flute; Stanley Drucker, principal clarinet; William Vacchiano, principal trumpet; and others who were such a colorful part of this very impressionable time of my life.

It was difficult at the time for me to imagine what working with Mr. Bernstein would be like. I was in such awe of him through what I had seen on his televised Young People's Concerts, hearing his recordings, going to his concerts, and hearing the tales that circulated among the players about this legend.

Musings on a Musical Journey

I was scheduled to play in one piece, *Phorion* by Lucas Foss, a cleverly written take-off on the *Preludium* to J.S. Bach's *E Major Violin Partita*. Although written for large orchestras, it contained a showy, technically challenging soprano saxophone part, which exposed the saxophone to the orchestra and the audience. Thinking about this giant who was to conduct, I found myself wondering if I was ready for this. I must admit to being terrified when he arrived at that first rehearsal.

Although the piece was a new contemporary work, it was relatively well-received by an occasionally stiff New York City audience. I was pleased with my part and Lenny seemed to like the results of the whole endeavor. Under the circumstances, we were all happy that it came together as well as it did. It was not an easy undertaking. Personally, I felt relieved that my part fit in as well as it did.

I always felt secure that Bernstein was never *in your face* with his conducting style. He gave us the freedom to individually interpret within his boundaries and the orchestra members appreciated that trait.

There were many recording sessions and television shows with Mr. Bernstein, especially during the late 1960s in New York City. They were all day and often back-to-back sessions. For me, however, the tours were the most memorable. Bernstein, ever the performer, was at his best while on tour. He thrived on playing a thrilling concert in a different concert hall every night for a new crowd. The momentum of the tours seemed to heighten his always star-like performances. No amount of exhaustion could stop him from pouring his heart out to the audiences.

The tour that made the biggest impression on me, however, included an episode that nearly sent me into cardiac arrest. In 1976, the orchestra embarked on a five-week tour of the United States and throughout Europe. This

Saxophone Troubadour

was not my first tour with Maestro Bernstein. The only pieces that I played for the tour repertoire were two Gershwin works, *Rhapsody in Blue* and *American in Paris* plus an encore piece also by Gershwin, the well-known *Second Piano Prelude*. This was a haunting, sultry orchestral arrangement from the library of Andre Kostelanetz's orchestra that featured the alto saxophone

Typically, instruments in symphony orchestras would be on-stage only when needed for the piece that is being done at any given time. Since each composition would have its unique array of instruments according to the composer's orchestration, players would arrive and/or leave the stage as needed. This is so as not to overcrowd the area with instruments that were not involved in any given piece. Not knowing if and when he would decide to perform the encore, *Second Prelude*, I felt it necessary to be on-stage just in case. Typical Bernstein, who noticed everything, probably understood that I was chomping at the bit to play my solo.

After a particular program early in the tour, he suggested to me that I would only need to be on-stage if the last work was *An American in Paris,* which I did have a part in. Similarly, if the program concluded with Copland's *Third Symphony*, the encore would be Copland's *Billy the Kid* (neither of which the saxophone was involved in). This seemed to be a simple solution and after three weeks of touring, all had gone according to plan.

For several performances, things went smoothly. From my perspective, the tour was wonderful and totally exciting. We played in Amsterdam, London, Brussels, Hamburg, Vienna, etc. Since concert tickets were in such great demand, we would often play in large arenas to satisfy the overflow audiences. There would sometimes be as many as 13,000 people at a single concert. It was truly exciting!

Musings on a Musical Journey

Then Came Berlin.

Everything about Berlin's concert was awesome. A capacity audience filled a vast cavern of a space called Deutschlandhalle. The high arched ceilings of the expansive structure seemed to bulge skyward with an overflow of elegantly dressed concertgoers. The backstage area was about the size of a football field. The numerous wardrobe, instrument, and equipment trunks that are part of a Philharmonic tour were spread out comfortably. Space and roominess were never problems here.

The concert consisted of William Schuman's *American Festival Overture*, Charles Ives' *The Unanswered Question*, Gershwin's *Rhapsody in Blue* (with Bernstein as both conductor and piano soloist) and closed with Copland's *Third Symphony*. In other words, no encore for me that night (or so I thought). It was an exceptionally easy evening for me since all I played was the *Rhapsody* and I was finished at intermission with no need to go back on stage for the second half.

At intermission, I changed from concert attire back to informal clothes and took off to meet an old friend at a German Brauhaus (beer hall, another highlight of the tour). It turned out that I left thirty minutes too soon.

After several drinks and some reminiscing, we returned to the backstage area just after the finish of Copland's Symphony. The resounding ovation seemed to be shaking the ribs of that colossal edifice. I had not been back more than a minute when the terror-stricken face of the personnel manager James Chambers greeted me. "Where have you been? I've been searching for you for the last thirty-five minutes! Lenny wants to do *the Prelude* as a first encore."

Saxophone Troubadour

Apparently, the maestro had decided this, in typical Bernstein fashion, just as he was going on stage to conduct the symphony. Since I had left just after it began, Mr. Chambers didn't have a chance to relay the information.

"Get your horn, forget the white coat, get on the stage quickly," he growled. Next, my sweating, trembling hands are grappling with the combination lock on my instrument trunk. After what seemed like an eternity, the horn was finally out and I'm praying for another minute of applause so I can at least get to my seat. Now my legs are pumping as if in a nightmare, feeling that every ounce of my energy is getting me nowhere.

I was about halfway across this empty backstage gridiron, streaking toward the goal line when it suddenly occurred to me that my prayer was not going to be answered. I was still running when I heard the familiar bass notes, a vamp-like intro to the *Prelude II*.

Just as my heart stops beating, I hear the most beautiful trumpet solo in the world. For a moment, I think it's all over, and this is what I'm hearing in the first moments of death. Gerard Schwarz, the principal trumpeter of the orchestra, got wind of the situation and played the alto saxophone part on his trumpet (most beautifully, I must add). I never stopped thanking Gerry for saving me from total heart failure on that night.

So now, how do I say "I'm sorry" to Leonard Bernstein? That question was answered when I got a penetrating leer from him that made me want to crawl into a pistachio shell. I reasoned that the most prudent thing to do was to say nothing. Maestro Bernstein, however, was not one to let things go so easily.

The next concert where *the Prelude* was to be played was in Vienna's Stadthalle six nights later. I got to my seat a little earlier than usual, determined to right the wrong with my best possible performance. So, what does he do? He makes the whole orchestra sit while *he* alone plays the encore on solo piano. I was never sure whether that was some sort of admonishment or not, but it was the only time that he did that.

As a side note, I learned another valuable lesson from Lenny. Early in the tour, we played at the Kennedy Center in Washington, DC. The date was May 23, 1976. At that concert, the encore piece was the *Prelude II*. Bernstein loved to acknowledge and give solo performers a bow. While standing, I carelessly let my saxophone dangle along my side. "Get the instrument up so they know what you played (and other unintelligible words)" came bellowing from the podium. From that day on, my horn was always held high in a gratitude-filled tribute to my favorite conductor.

Leopold Stokowski

To musicians who worked with him, Maestro Leopold Stokowski was infamously known as *Stoki*. Contrary to our frequent addressing of Maestro Leonard Bernstein by *Lenny,* Stokowski's nickname was not used in his presence. Because Leopold was a man who prided himself on being dignified and well cultivated, I can only assume that the nickname Stoki was a product of the irreverence of orchestral musicians but used with fondness.

I had never before heard of any other prominent conductor being given an informal nickname. One could never imagine Arturo Toscanini, Serge Koussevitsky, Sir Thomas Beecham, Otto Klemperer, or a host of other famous present or past conductors referred to in less than respectful or dignified manners.

Maestro Stokowski's physical trademark was his silvery/gray hair that was seldom unkempt in public. He prided himself on his unique handsomeness and his

Saxophone Troubadour

statuesque poise, plus a very striking stare akin to a laser beam. He seemed to favor photos of himself that were of his profile that emphasized his Polish/Eastern European facial features. And even though he was born in England, he bore no trace of a British accent.

Stoki's credits were many and he was a major force in the music world during the majority of the 20th Century. His artistic successes were plentiful, but most notable were his work with the Philadelphia Orchestra and movie making in Hollywood. The movie *Fantasia* which featured him conducting *The Rite of Spring* and him shaking hands with Mickey Mouse are well-known cinematic scenes even to this day. His list of credits in his very industrious and innovative life is voluminous, and these are well documented in many volumes of musicians' biographies and memoirs.

My association with Maestro Stokowski started in 1964 when I began playing the bass clarinet, utility clarinet, and saxophone with the American Symphony Orchestra. The ASO was formed by the Maestro when he was 80 years old. It followed the New York Philharmonic as the resident orchestra of Carnegie Hall in 1962. This was as a result of the NY Phil's move to its new home in the then-called Avery Fisher Hall at Lincoln Center. That move gave the American Symphony the opening to become a part of the prestigious Carnegie Hall legacy.

Maestro Stokowski was an energetic, spunky chap who managed to keep a very busy schedule throughout his life. His conducting years took him well into his nineties. He was forever the showman and was an expert at using flamboyant techniques to enhance his performances.

Lighting had to be just right to show off his glowing silvery/white crown of hair and many staging effects were used to bring attention to his free beautifully expressive hands that never held a baton. Yes, he never used a baton but brought every nuance to life solely with smooth hand gestures.

Music reviewers often referred to his hands as the secret to the uniqueness of the string section sound he created. His smooth arm movements were his trademarks and no one could deny that he certainly elicited magic in this respect. The slightest movement of a palm or a wrist inflection could somehow make every dynamic come to life with a shimmering satin-like quality. His fingers seemed to be arranging palettes of sound colors into a delicate mosaic.

Another aspect of The Maestro's persona was what many considered to be a contrived accent. Having been proud of his Polish heritage he developed a rather thick Eastern European-type speech pattern when he spoke English that baffled those who came into contact with him. Since he was born in London and spent the majority of his life living in the United States one could only wonder what and where the Eastern European accent originated.

His motto was "DO BETTER" which he would constantly preach to players, especially young ones. It came out as "DO BETTA, DO BETTA". The American Symphony softball team uniform consisted of T-Shirts that displayed that saying. I guess we couldn't be good enough even on the ball field.

On rehearsal days Stoki would arrive one-half hour before downbeat and plant himself on his podium stool. Like the beacon from a lighthouse, he seemed to hone in on every player as they entered and he watched as they prepared themselves for the day's work. He was very cognizant of the way his players warmed up and looked over their parts. If a player was arriving at his seat in the last minute before rehearsals, the maestro was aware and often would make sure the person was aware that he knew.

Saxophone Troubadour

He was an educator in many respects and cared about grooming young players with good professional disciplines. Sometimes this was done at the cost of humiliating them in front of the orchestra. I always felt sorry for whoever the ax would fall on and must admit that I was constantly on the alert to make sure it didn't come to me.

I tried to keep an awareness of how and when he was looking my way. I had the feeling that the laser ray of his stare would emit a glaring beam. You can be sure I made it a point to not be late for rehearsals. In that respect, it was a good lesson, albeit a bit intimidating.

Some amusing stories came out of incidents that took place during rehearsals and concerts.

One of the most famous happened during one of his three premiere performances of the Charles Ives *4th Symphony* in 1964. In typical Stokowski fashion, he was fearless in going after the most complicated works and seeing them through to public performance. He was the first to premiere many famous composers' works including those of Rachmaninoff, Mahler, Hovhaness, Seigmeister, Varese, Schoenberg, and the aforementioned Ives *4th Symphony*.

The Ives *4th Symphony* was as complicated as they get from a conductor's viewpoint in that it required the coordination of not only the principal conductor but of two associate conductors. The individual parts required much technical skill as well as the ability of the individual players to keep track of the direction coming from three different stage positions. In any case, it is a piece that invites disaster and in one particular instance, that was exactly what happened.

During one complicated exchange of tempos and transition, the orchestra fell completely apart and the individual players had no idea of where the next set of notes should come from. That is, except for the bass clarinetist,

Musings on a Musical Journey

Jimmy Abato, who continued to play by improvising in the style of Ives while the rest of the approximately 100 players came to a grinding halt.

Maestro Stokowski in his ever-present, capture-the-moment showmanship went right along as if nothing was out of place and continued to conduct the lone player, improvising right along with him. He emphasized sweeping gestures with his trademark hand gestures while his flowing crown of silvery hair swirled as if it were all a part of the drama in the actual score.

Somehow the extemporizing led to the next section when one of the secondary conductors called out the next starting place and brought the whole orchestra back into the real world. Decidedly one of the most memorable hold-your-breath moments in symphonic history.

Another memorable blooper event occurred at an ASO concert in Carnegie Hall during the encore piece of a regular subscription series. Stokie did various arrangements and transcriptions of works that he tailored for the orchestra. One such piece was the *Toccata and Fugue* by J.S. Bach, a work originally written for organ.

The composition opened with a series of disjointed figures that were very much designed to be played in a flurry of notes to allow an organist to fly over the keys in an individual extemporaneous flow. Great to show off the technical capabilities of a powerful solitary organ player but a bit complicated to get an entire orchestra to come together even under the great Stokowski's leadership.

This particular concert was nearing the time of Stokowski's 85th birthday and to commemorate it *Life Magazine* sent a photographer who was given permission to actually be on the stage while the concert was in progress. The photographer was thoroughly professional and certainly stayed hidden and in fact, was hardly noticed

Saxophone Troubadour

throughout the performance of several pieces in the main portion of the concert. He would move unobtrusively along the back wall of the stage and subtly take his shots between the double basses and percussion players while remaining well out of the way.

I must first explain that the Stokowski arrangement of this work showed off the most dramatic and flamboyant side of the maestro's conducting prowess. His trademark hands got their full workout with sweeping gestures and swirling fingers. His silver-grey hair gave off a display of brilliance. Stokie was in his glory whenever he conducted this work. So even though this was the encore piece on this program he gave it considerable preparation time.

He spent more rehearsal time on this work than any of the other main pieces on the program. Stokowski wanted to end the program in a shower of radiance to display to the world his fiery dramatic and youthful presence even at 85 years of age.

Even with all of the rehearsing, the piece did not really come together and both the conductor and orchestra never quite felt comfortable in pulling it off. The main works in the concert otherwise were a good display of typical classical masterworks that were well played and well received by the audience. Then came the encore.

Stokowski's first swooping gesture was dramatically obvious but quickly turned into a cacophony of sounds by an unprepared orchestra. Maestro Stokowski immediately brought us to a halt and decided to start over. Maybe because of the shock of it all, the second start came out more cacophonous than the first, at which point we were directed to stop again.

This time the Maestro gave another swooping gesture only this time at the photographer to get the hell off the stage. He followed it by a long silence to give the poor magazine guy time to be noticed and slither off to the backstage and out of sight. As he was leaving, he looked at Stokie with a sheepish look of disbelief as if to say "Who me? What did I do"? Stokie responded with a dramatic Hollywood facial glare that could be read from every seat in Carnegie Hall. His Hollywood training prepared him well for a moment such as this.

The shaken orchestra along with a frustrated Stokie started over for the third time. AND yes, another confusion of notes, only this time we were out of excuses and had to continue.

If we thought the Maestro's glare at the photographer was embarrassing, this one was as if some 90 plus daggers came flying out of his eyes at every player on stage. At the end of this catastrophe, we all slithered off the stage making sure not to be anywhere in the Maestro's presence.

Pierre Boulez

From 1971 through 1977 Pierre Boulez was appointed director of the New York Philharmonic. He was certainly among the conductors whom I highly respected. His knowledge, conducting, and understanding of the modern concert repertoire of the 20th century were arguably the greatest of his time. The hallmark of his extraordinary musicianship in my opinion was his ability to hear out-of-tune playing at the most critical of decibels. When he detected a less than perfect combination of pitches, he would whistle the correct tuning with uncanny certainty that was nothing short of amazing.

Boulez was always the polished gentleman and seldom would raise his voice. As a result, his rehearsals were very orderly and effective, especially when he conducted his specialty pieces. His podium demeanor was serious and to the point, always solely into the business of making music. He would very often come to rehearsals smartly dressed in a suit and tie and presented himself in a suave manner.

Among works such as *The Rite of Spring, Miraculous Mandarin, Wozzeck,* and others of mid 20th Century fame that he directed with the most minute details, he was able to exact the musician's unmitigated attention.

Directly the opposite of Leonard Bernstein, Boulez's conducting technique was very compact and not given to big sweeping gestures. His method was very tight and angular, often with his left arm dangling at his side while his right hand would give very rhythmic concise movements. His beat was very clear and to the point, without any unnecessary ostentation. In short, he was always the technician and seldom the showman. As a result, reviewers of his performances would sometimes feel that they were lacking in emotional appeal.

I was fortunate to have had several performances under Pierre Boulez and many were very memorable. The one that stands out was in April of 1969. I was asked to play alto clarinet in Igor Stravinsky's *Symphonies of Wind Instruments.* This was the original scoring of the work and employed the seldom-used alto clarinet in G. Since I was used very often as an extra clarinetist as well as saxophonist with the orchestra during that era, I was given the unenviable task of playing that somewhat unusual instrument. Although it was a member of the clarinet family its timbre was unlike any of the others and took some getting used to.

As it turned out, I easily took to the instrument and after extensive practice familiarizing myself with its idiosyncrasies found that it had a beautiful dark and mellow sound quality that I found quite attractive. An additional perk was that the alto clarinet part to the

Musings on a Musical Journey

Symphonies of Wind Instruments was heavily solo laden and very lyrically written. In actuality, it was a fun part to play because of its extensive exposure.

After my personal preparation, I felt secure and excited to get to the first concert. Rehearsals went well and even though Boulez was not one to say much in the way of compliments, it was apparent that he was happy with the result as it was coming together. Then came the first performance on April 3rd, 1969.

Things went very smoothly, and I was quite pleased with the results of what seemed to be a very tight performance. After getting the usual complimentary solo bow at the conclusion I proceeded to the instrument room feeling elated at the proceedings knowing that my work paid off.

And then, the voice of James Chambers, the New York Philharmonic's personnel manager, came over the room intercom. "Al Regni, please come up to the office."

Oh, oh, I thought, *what could this be about?*

"Go up to the Maestro's room, he would like to see you," Mr. Chambers said.

After a knock and short wait at the director's door, I was invited in by a smiling Mr. Boulez. He was quite relaxed and after a few pleasantries, he remarked, "Your playing was very good, but tell me, how did you come to play an E-flat on your opening chord note instead of the written F?"

After a brief thought, I replied, "I don't see how I could have done that because that would be quite a different fingering to produce so high a note and I'm sure I didn't do that."

The opening note that I played was part of a 13-note atonal cluster that was dramatic and loud. The fact that he could single out any one of the notes was awesome. Mr.

Saxophone Troubadour

Chambers who was present, chimed in "Perhaps you heard a resultant tone." **

Mr. Boulez's quick and incredulous reply was "No, I know this piece!"

At that, I apologized and said that whatever the problem was I would fix it. Immediately returning to the instrument room I took out the alto clarinet and started experimenting to determine what possibly could have happened.

It took about five minutes of playing the note in question when I realized that an idiosyncrasy of the alto clarinet is that high notes can be overblown to produce a higher part of the harmonic series. *Nothing like on the job training*, I thought!

Before the performance on the following day, I again went up to the conductor's room and explained what happened. He was gracious in letting me know in his grinning smile that spoke, *I told you so*. I was happy that he was so understanding.

At the performance, he looked straight at me just before that chord, and when he heard the *right* sound he gave me a wink and nod. Pierre had his very human moments.

The Prospective Encounters were a series of concerts which took place at New York's historic Cooper Union where Lincoln gave his presidential acceptance speech. A second series was held at Philharmonic Hall at Lincoln Center and known as the *Rug Concerts*. At these concerts, the first-floor seats of the entire hall were removed, and the audience sat on a rug-covered floor with pillows. This gave a very informal, relaxed feel to the concert atmosphere and for the most part, was greatly accepted by the audiences.

**A resultant tone is when two notes are played simultaneously, and a third tone is sometimes produced.

Musings on a Musical Journey

At one of the *Cooper Union Prospective Encounters Concerts,* I was involved in a performance of the Anton Webern Quartet, *Opus 22 for Violin, Clarinet, Piano and Tenor Saxophone.* The players were Enrico Di Cecco, Violin; Stanley Drucker, Clarinet; Paul Jacobs, Piano, and me, Tenor Saxophone. The piece is a very short scantily written work with an abundance of transparency.

These concerts were not only meant to acquaint audiences with contemporary compositions that were seldom heard but to explain and dissect the music to be better understood. At this particular concert, Boulez asked me at the concert (without any previous warning) if I would play eight measures of what he termed the main melodic line.

I had no idea that it was a main melodic line up to that point. Not having had a chance to even think about it, I found myself playing this fragment hoping that it was what was intended. It must have been acceptable because Messrs. Boulez gave me a warm smile when I finished.

Ordinarily, this would have been a typical New York performance moment. What made it extraordinary was that seated in the front row were Aaron Copland, Leonard Bernstein, Elliot Carter, and Lucas Foss, four of America's leading musicians and exponents of contemporary music. Events such as these were oftentimes good confidence builders for the performers. This, fortunately for me, was one of those occasions.

I enjoyed playing for Pierre Boulez and was sorry that his tenure with the orchestra was short, only lasting six years. He probably came to The New York Philharmonic before its audiences were ready for the avant-garde music of the mid 20th Century, which he often championed. A loss for New York in my opinion.

Chapter 8
A Few Tour Experiences 1968 – 2012

When starting out back in the 1960s I never expected that my career choice would allow me to see so much of the world, but I was indeed fortunate to have had many unforgettable experiences. The bulk of travel was because of my association with the New York Philharmonic. There were other wonderful tours with The Metropolitan Opera Orchestra. These included the National Symphony, the New York City Ballet Orchestra, the Baltimore Symphony, the Los Angeles Philharmonic, Israel Philharmonic, Rotterdam Philharmonic, St. Petersburg (Russia) Philharmonic, the American Symphony Orchestra, Odessa Philharmonic, Leningrad Philharmonic, the Steve Reich Ensemble and a fabulous four-month tour with Liza Minelli.

Playing the saxophone in a symphony orchestra has some very definite advantages. Orchestras do not, as a matter of course, have saxophonists on their regular roster; but many orchestras that travel often hire a player in New York City to accompany them on their U.S. tours. This is because the symphonic repertoire is limited in its use of the saxophone.

Big works that do incorporate the sax such as Mussorgsky's Pictures at an Exhibition, Rachmaninoff's Symphonic Dances, Ravel's Bolero, Prokofiev's Romeo and

Musings on a Musical Journey

Juliet plus several others are blockbuster pieces that show off the mastery of the ensembles. Because of this, they are favorites with audiences around the world, and fortunately for me, they all contained saxophone parts.

1970 was a particularly exciting year because it was my first international tour with the New York Philharmonic. It was that much more thrilling because it featured Leonard Bernstein and Seiji Ozawa as co-conductors along with the some of the world's most prominent and legendary orchestral musicians. To be traveling, performing, hearing their stories first-hand, and just rubbing shoulders with these giants was more than a dream come true.

I had been hired to play alto saxophone in Modest Mussorgsky's Pictures at an Exhibition. Second, only to his opera Boris Godunov, this was his most famous work. This piece was originally composed for solo piano and later realized for a large orchestra by Maurice Ravel. Lucky for me, it features a prominent solo for the alto saxophone in a movement entitled The Old Castle. Considered to be among the most beautiful and exposed solos in the entire classical repertoire, it is a lyrical dream that embodies the lushness and warmth of the alto saxophone.

To perform this as part of the New York Philharmonic's historic tour of Japan was indeed an honor that required me to be at the top of my game. I was determined therefore to be as ready as possible when the downbeat came. Pictures was conducted by Maestro Ozawa and I was additionally required to play clarinet in Gustav Mahler's 7th Symphony. This was equally thrilling because it was conducted by Maestro Bernstein at the height of his prowess. Having been a part of these performances I still consider it to be among the biggest thrills of my entire career.

Saxophone Troubadour

Seiji Ozawa was unfortunately not held in high esteem by many Japanese because of his recent divorce from pianist Kyoko Edo. Many Japanese felt that she, along with her influential high society family, was a big factor in Ozawa's quick rise to fame. As a result, his appearances were accepted with a measure of skepticism. The quality of his performances however rectified that with praise from the critics. I was especially pleased to read some favorable reviews for the saxophone solo that appeared in various Japanese periodicals.

Leonard Bernstein on the other hand was a well-known hero of the Japanese as well as to lovers of the entire music world. His mere appearance elicited an aura of splendor before he even raised the baton. LB was a master at making his presence ignite a room.

His demeanor was a combination of New York high society and Hollywood glamour that was truly electrifying. He was not shy about flaunting his qualities even though some thought it was over the top *chutzpah*.**

Traveling by airplane from New York City to Tokyo, Japan in 1970 meant a layover in Anchorage, Alaska for refueling. This was quite nice and refreshing because at that time tobacco smoking was permitted on airplanes and included cigars and pipes as well as cigarettes. Getting off the airplane and outside into the fresh, breathable Alaskan air for an hour was a wonderful break.

Traveling with me, was my ex-wife Charlotte who had the misfortune of sitting between me smoking cigarettes and Stanley Drucker smoking cigars for most of the way. I can still picture that poor woman gagging for 16 hours.

There were no smoking-free spaces on a chartered flight in

** Chutzpah is a Yiddish term having to do with shameless but admirable audacity.

Musings on a Musical Journey

1970, so, there was a constant saturation of tobacco smoke that permeated every crevice of the aircraft. How some of us managed to stay fairly healthy today without a major related disease is something of a miracle.

In 1970, the New York Philharmonic Japan Tour could be described as a traveling men's club. Outside of a few accompanying orchestra wives, there were only two performing female members who were on the tour. Card games were rampant throughout the plane and trying to get a few winks of sleep was not possible amidst the constant snapping of card shuffling, occasional outbursts of hilarity, and an abundance of alcohol use. It reminded me of my youth in upstate Binghamton, New York when I would play gigs at the local Moose Club and had witnessed the camaraderie among the all-male members.

Arriving in Osaka, Japan was a particularly exciting time at this early period of my career. It was my first trip to Japan, and I still consider it among my favorite countries to visit, as well as to perform in.

On this first tour, we played in Osaka, Kyoto, Fukuoka, Tokyo, Nagoya, and Sapporo on Hokkaido, the most northern of the five Japanese islands. At every venue, we were treated like royalty in the typically warm and gracious hospitality of the Japanese people.

The opening night concert was in Osaka in the spacious Festival Hall which was attached to the Osaka Grand hotel where the entire orchestra was in residence. At the time, the Osaka Grand Hotel was the best in town. Every room was tasteful in design and the ballrooms were spectacularly adorned.

The opening night reception was held in the main ballroom which contained an impressive swooping stairway that was reminiscent of the one at Tara from Gone with the Wind. Gold leaf panels everywhere and the massive chandelier that hung from above gave one a feeling of unabashed luxury.

At the conclusion of the SRO concert the entire New York Philharmonic and many Japanese luminaries flooded into the immense ballroom for an elegant reception. This was a white tie and tails event. The incredibly adorned Japanese women, many of whom were in colorful traditional kimono attire, gave the space a radiant glow. It was truly a memorable occasion for Japanese/American relations and the spirit of camaraderie was ubiquitous.

The entire orchestra along with hundreds of people were shoulder to shoulder in the spacious ballroom. Mr. Brook and his wife Alice were situated directly in the center of the dance floor. Paige had broken his ankle just before the beginning of the tour. Because he was on crutches, he was unable to move very quickly or smoothly. This is an important point to make in consideration of what occurred during Maestro Bernstein's grand entrance.

Without warning, the lights dimmed and a spotlight appeared at the top of the swooping staircase. As an immediate hushed silence fell over the crowd Leonard Bernstein appeared accompanied by his twenty-something-year-old valet portraying a dramatic image. This was a Hollywood scene that was as memorable as any that was ever filmed.

Lenny was adorned in white tie and tails with a black velvet cape lined in blood-red satin. His silvery flowing hair reflected a shocking glow that sparkled. His valet was decked-out in a white dinner jacket and was equally magnificent with a crop of golden blond hair that was a compliment to the colorful array of the couple. This scene could not have been surpassed in its extraordinary choreography. Truly a sight to behold.

Musings on a Musical Journey

As the scene unfolded one of the orchestra members exclaimed, "Look out, here comes Batman and Rubin!"

At this point, the crowd on the dance floor gave the impression of the Red Sea dividing. It was a hasty move on the part of the many bodies, except for Paige and Alice Brook who were slowed by Paige's hobbling on crutches. As a result, he and Alice were the first to be greeted by the maestro in the center of an emptied dance floor.

Being greeted by Mr. Bernstein meant being passionately kissed. He continued through the massive crowd embracing everyone within his reach. Kissing between members of the same sex was not as prevalent in 1970 except for perhaps the European cultures. It certainly had not arrived in the formality of Japanese society but, since it was Bernstein, it was readily accepted.

As a result, the Japanese paparazzi were all over the scene and Paige was rewarded with a front-page photo of the encounter in the following day's newspapers. Mr. Brook being the good-natured individual that he was, took it in high spirits.

The excitement of the tour was not confined to the concert hall or the magnificent cities. An exciting event that took place during our stop in Tokyo was a pre-arranged softball game between the New York Philharmonic Penguins and the RHK Symphony of Japan. The game took place in none other than Tokyo's Giant's Stadium. This field is akin to Yankee Stadium in the Bronx and the most heralded of sports locations in Japan. The Japanese orchestra took their baseball very seriously and made their initial appearance as if it was a national championship game. They trotted onto the field in an orderly single file decked out in professional uniforms.

The New York Philharmonic Penguins, on the other hand, hobbled onto the field in their short-sleeved

Saxophone Troubadour

sweatshirts and a variety of leg coverings that the Japanese took exception to. They provided us with and insisted we wear suitable knee-length baseball pants and socks so as not to insult the legacy of Giant's Stadium.

After witnessing us over-sized Americans sporting Japanese sized baseball knickers that were well above our knees, they must have had second thoughts about preserving Giant Stadium's legacy.

A sight that is well preserved in my brain is Leonard Bernstein dressed in an immaculate white sweater, pants, and shoes coaching third base with the same kind of pizzazz as if he were conducting a one-hundred-piece symphony orchestra. He was crouched over with his hands on his knees shouting typical baseball banter. He knew how to inspire magic even on the ball field.

Seiji Ozawa, our alternate conductor, was playing shortstop with a bit too much exuberance. Unfortunately, he wrenched his back sliding into second base and was unable to conduct that evening's performance. We all tended to forget that we were over-the-hill athletes, but somehow we survived without too many bumps and bruises. As the game proceeded to become more and more competitive it was decided to end in a three-to-three tie to avoid any dissent and to maintain good relations.

Our umpire for this game was Japan's illustrious Sadaharu Oh who even to this day, is the leading home run hitter in the world. His record of 868 career home runs exceeds both Hank Aaron's 755 and Barry Bonds 762.

He took a turn at bat and shattered our expectations by popping out to third base. We, however, were certainly honored to be in the presence of Japan's legendary and good-natured Hall-of-Famer who was the pride of the Yomiuri Giants of Bunkyo, Tokyo, Japan.

Musings on a Musical Journey

My first experience of acquiring a taste for sushi happened on this trip and I haven't looked back. It was then that I also acquired a taste for teriyaki and Shabu-shabu among several other lesser-known dishes. One of the most outstanding foods was the Hokkaido salmon which is in a class by itself. This was a wonderful added joy to a fabulous tour hosted by the Japanese people, who are among the most congenial and hospitable in world travel. This tour and several afterward confirmed that point over and over.

It has been particularly exciting traveling with foreign orchestras. The Israel Philharmonic was exciting in more ways than one. This orchestra is a group of fabulous virtuosi and warm friendly types that were quick to introduce themselves in a most welcoming way. Because it is a self-governing orchestra, I remember most fondly meeting various members who would say, "Hello I'm Itzhak, I'm the assistant manager." or "Hello I'm Saul, I'm the assistant manager."

I must have met 50 assistant managers and as a result, would joke with them. My question was, "Where are the rank and file? You all seem to be managers."

As would be expected the security was of major concern. Traveling on El Al airlines was an experience beyond anything I could ever have imagined. When joining the orchestra at Kennedy Airport in New York it took me close to one hour of intense interrogation before I was allowed on the plane.

Every city where we landed was heavily protective of the orchestra. The landing in Naples, Italy was a most memorable experience. After landing, the aircraft parked on a runway as far away from the terminal as was possible. As soon as the plane came to a stop a fleet of military busses, armored cars, and a helicopter appeared around and over us. A regiment of Italian soldiers immediately encircled as we boarded the busses. Anyone carrying a bag or even an instrument was searched before boarding. I remember one of the musicians remarking "Here we are, The sitting ducks Israel Phil!"

One of the Italian performances which took place at the beautiful outdoor stadium venue in Pompei was heavily protected by armed soldiers during the concert. Playing in France was also a high-security stop since 1988 was a period of much unrest, particularly in Paris. Terrorists were placing bombs under parked cars, and it was scary to just walk on the sidewalks. All of the concerts on that particular tour were exciting however since they were conducted by everyone's favorite, Leonard Bernstein.

On one occasion I finished a two-week tour in Louisville, Kentucky with the Israel Phil and was able to go directly to the airport and connect flights to Athens, Greece to join the New York Phil on a three-week tour of Europe. This was not unusual for a conductor but highly unusual for a mere saxophonist.

Playing in so many incredible concert halls, such as The Vienna Opera House, Tchaikovsky Hall in Moscow, Detroit's Orchestra Hall, Royal Albert Hall in London, Amsterdam's Concertgebouw, the Beijing Concert Hall, North Korea's beautiful concert space, and of course, New York's Carnegie Hall are among the standouts. If I had to choose a favorite, it would have to be right here in the USA and that would be Detroit's Orchestra Hall. Playing there with the Rotterdam Philharmonic in 1987 was a thrill in itself, but the magnificence of that space was in my opinion the concert hall jewel of the world.

In the 1980s Detroit was not the most attractive city in the country since it had been subjected to upheaval in the way of riots and unrest for many prior years. Orchestra Hall, located on Woodward Avenue was in a very torn up area and additionally had gone through a shaky history with unsettled financial problems. For those reasons it was nearly demolished and was fortunately saved by private and public funding much the same as Carnegie Hall in New York.

The splendor of this Art-Deco building is only surpassed by the perfect acoustics of the concert hall. This is not only a universal agreement by musicians but was scientifically acknowledged by many experts in the field of acoustics. My experience of playing the saxophone solo in Rachmaninoff's Symphonic Dances at Orchestra Hall was that the sound simply floated out effortlessly, with incredible natural amplification. We played the previous night at New York's Carnegie Hall and having had the chance to rate them side by side I would have to give my vote to Detroit's Orchestra Hall.

Touring with the Leningrad Philharmonic was a thrilling as well as a nerve-racking experience at times. There was one memorable occasion, perhaps it was because of a communication breakdown between me and the contractor.

I had been given a concert schedule by the manager well before the tour began and nowhere on the itinerary was a concert at Washington, D.C.'s Kennedy Center scheduled for a Sunday afternoon. After playing the previous Saturday night at Carnegie Hall in New York City, which I was led to believe was the final concert of the tour, the contractor presented me with a plane ticket for the following morning for a Sunday afternoon 3 pm concert at The Kennedy Center in Washington, D.C.

When I told the contractor that I was unable to travel with the orchestra because of an engagement I had booked with a chamber music group at Alice Tully Hall in New York for that Sunday morning and evening, he fell short of having a stroke. Since I had already rehearsed for the Alice Tully

Saxophone Troubadour

Hall concert it was too late to employ a replacement. The Sunday morning New York gig was a dress rehearsal at 10 am with a concert scheduled for 8 pm.

I knew that the shuttle flight from New York's La Guardia airport to Washington, D.C.'s Reagan airport was a 45-minute flight and since there was a 1:30 pm flight I could be in D.C. by 2:30 pm. When I explained this to the manager he reluctantly agreed. I did not play until the second half of the program and would not need to be on stage until 3:45. Fortunately, things worked out and it all fell into place, complete with a Russian flagged limousine picking me up and driving to the Kennedy Center.

The sweaty-faced manager met me at the stage door at 3:20 pm and the first half of the program still had 25 minutes to go before intermission. The piece that employed the saxophone was Sergei Prokofiev's Alexander Nevsky, a large work for orchestra and chorus which was a rousing finish to the Russian tour and thankfully, my last gig with the orchestra.

The next time I was hired to play with them was several years later when they became the St. Petersburg Orchestra. I made sure that the schedule was well communicated at that time. Incidentally, I was able to get to the 6 pm shuttle and make it back to New York with a modicum of time to spare before the 8 pm Alice Tully concert.

Playing at the United Nations is always an interesting opportunity to witness the workings of world harmony (or disharmony). One memorable performance there with the Los Angeles Philharmonic featured the conductor Zubin Mehta reprimanding the delegates for their inability to keep peace in the world. His over-the-top scolding was not well received by the audience but did not deter Mr. Mehta from letting them know what he thought.

Musings on a Musical Journey

His lecture consisted of telling them that Music and the Arts promoted more world harmony than all of their proceedings combined. I did not notice any of the delegates leaving the hall but the deafening silence in the room spoke volumes. I also felt that his choice of playing a piece that featured loud cacophonous music was not appropriate, especially after the embarrassing tongue-lashing he had just dealt out.

Sightseeing is very tempting on trips, especially in towns that are not popular concert stops. One very interesting and beautiful destination is Hanover, Germany. The incredible labyrinth in the Herrenhausen Gardens is one of the most popular sightseeing attractions there.

A group from the New York Philharmonic and I decided to visit the venue. I was not aware of the possibilities of getting lost in all the twists and turns involved and as a result, lost touch with my group. Talk about panic: I suddenly found myself alone in a winding maze of endless green shrubbery. Sweating at every wrong turn, I somehow managed to free myself from unintentional self-imposed captivity.

The next problem was getting back to the hotel for the 7 pm transport of the orchestra to the concert hall. This was worrisome since it was now 5 pm and I had no idea where I was, could not speak any German, did not know which bus to take and the worst part was I couldn't even remember the name of the hotel.

This was 1976 in the days before cell phones and my chance of making a call on a German public phone was not remotely possible. There were no taxis and the only thing left to do was to take my chances with a public bus.

I decided to take the first bus that came along with the hope that by some miracle a guardian angel would get me out of this mess. My guardian angels showed up in the form of Elliot and Helen Carter

Mr. Elliot Carter was the legendary American composer who was traveling with the New York Philharmonic as a featured artist representing the best of American music on the 1976 Bicentennial tour with the orchestra. It was my good fortune that he and his wife happened to be on that particular bus, at that particular time, or I could have been lost in Hannover, Germany for a good long time, not to mention missing the concert.

It was an experience that taught me to never take for granted the intricate logistics of traveling in a foreign country especially where I could not speak the language.

Being with an extraordinary group of artists was a distinct perc as every day was a learning experience. The bicentennial tour of 1976 was a particularly fine example. I became friendly with the associate first oboist of the orchestra, Ronald Roseman. Mr. Roseman was a first-class virtuoso as well as a fine man and it was an honor to play duets with him on several occasions.

Because we both played on the same repertoire, we shared the same breaks between pieces. To fill in the time, we would play duets for flute and oboe. This was a particular treat for me in that I had no other opportunities to play the flute on the tour since I was employed as a saxophonist.

A near miss occurred for me during one backstage duet session. We were doing a live television broadcast of a concert in Mannheim, Germany. It was a long intermission between the individual pieces because of live one-on-one interviews taking place. Ron and I decided to get in a duet session and were wrapped up in it when we were suddenly interrupted by French hornist Aubrey Facenda.

Musings on a Musical Journey

He casually asked me "Aren't you supposed to be on stage?" He added, "They are starting Rhapsody in Blue," which was a piece that I played on. Having been so wrapped up in the enjoyment of playing with Ron I had completely lost track of time. Fortunately, I was suited up in white tie and tails and in the flash of an instant made it to the stage.

Two factors saved the day. First, this was a TV live concert performance and the stage was completely dark except a spotlight on the solo clarinetist, Stanley Drucker, who had just started the famous opening glissando of the Rhapsody. Second, I had a few seconds to get in my seat before I had anything to play that could be readily noticed on camera. This was a near-miss moment, and I breathed a sigh of relief when the piece ended without incident.

A four-month tour with Liza Minnelli was the source of some very memorable experiences. Playing in Sydney, Australia comes to mind as one that could have proven to be an unpleasant recollection had it worked out differently.

Chip Jackson the bass player, Kenny Berger the baritone saxophonist, and I were invited to go for a sailing jaunt on the magnificent Sydney harbor. I had very little experience at being on a small sailboat and no experience at all being on such a mammoth bay. We were invited to go on this cruise by a local Australian trumpeter whom we had met during our week-long stay in Sydney. Chip was an experienced sailor, but Kenny and I were real landlubbers.

We could not have chosen a more perfect day for this event and as a result, we managed to be on the water for a good six hours. I was enthralled with the sights of the famous Sydney Opera House, sailing across to the picturesque zoo with hopping kangaroos, drifting past the pristine beaches, witnessing the many surfers, and, of course, seeing the Sydney skyline. It was indeed a day to remember. Later that evening, playing for the Liza show, however, was not a pleasant memory and one that's hard to forget.

I was thoroughly invigorated from the day's activities, or so I thought, and it was after the show began that evening that the effect of sailing reared its terrifying face. I had never experienced the sensations of inner-ear or sea-legs as they are referred to, but I was sure made aware of them at that performance.

The stage set-up for Liza's show consisted of a variety of different levels of risers to seat the on-stage twelve-piece band. I was one of three saxophonists seated on three different heights. Kenny Berger was to my left on a low riser that sat two feet off of the floor, I was seated next to him on a riser that sat four feet off the floor, and tenor saxophonist, Frank Perowsky sat to my right on a riser that sat six feet off of the floor. The band stage set was a very modern, abstract, artsy design.

As soon as the curtain rose, I knew something was wrong. An audience of 1200 people seemed to be 3000 people. The crowd looked as if they were a field of vibrating cabbage heads. Also, the riser where I sat felt like it was going to cave in at any moment. Since we were required to stand at various parts of the act it was terrifying to think that the riser would not support the weight of our bodies. It was truly a creepy, scary feeling.

I yelled backstage to the stage manager to get under the riser and see what was going on. He assured me that all was fine, but I was convinced that the riser was going to collapse. I even refused to stand as part of the required stage scene movements to the dismay of Ms. Minnelli. I asked Kenny Berger who was seated next to me if he was feeling the same thing and he agreed. We both were in a state of utter panic.

Musings on a Musical Journey

At the intermission, Kenny and I stalked over to the stage manager and let him know we were not happy about the situation. He threw up his hands, leaped up onto the riser, and proceeded to jump up and down on it. I would estimate his weight at 250 pounds, and we were amazed that the structure did not budge. Now we all knew something was amiss.

Chip Jackson knew at that moment that we were experiencing inner-ear problems as a result of our day on the water. I believe that the glow from the redness of our faces must have added an extra texture to the many lights on stage during the second half of the performance. Somehow, we managed to get through the rest of the show even though we were quite embarrassed.

One of my favorite bandmates on the Liza tour was percussionist Michael Hinton. Michael and I spent much of our free time hanging out, exploring the sights but mostly going to arcades to play Pac-Man, the most popular electronic game in the 1980s. He was an energetic cheerful sort who was also prone to multitasking. Whenever he was not on the bandstand, he would be wearing an earpiece and preoccupied listening and still be fully aware of what was going on around him while carrying on a conversation. I came to find out that Mike was using every minute away from playing the shows to listen to a constant stream of recorded Japanese language lessons.

We were on a four-month tour and since he would be meeting the parents of his Japanese wife for the first time, he was determined to show them that a young Jewish man could master the language and culture of their country. During the third month of the tour, we arrived in Japan and his studies paid off. The parents met him dressed in traditional Japanese kimonos and were very impressed with his efforts. He was wholeheartedly accepted into the family.

Saxophone Troubadour

While traveling in Australia we had a week-long stay in Adelaide, which was one of my all-time favorite stops. Arriving there from Melbourne very late on a weekday evening Mike and I decided we were hungry and wanted to get a bite to eat. Since our hotel was located on the outskirts of town there were no available restaurants open at that time. We hailed a cab and directed the driver to take us to a "good restaurant" where we could find a hearty early morning breakfast.

Adelaide is the capital of South Australia and one of the country's largest and most beautiful cities. Since it has a reputation for producing some of the finest foods and wines in the country, we thought our chances of finding a spot would be good even in the wee hours. The cab driver assured us he could take us to just the place we were looking for. When we arrived at the driver's destination, I began to think that "good restaurant" might be code words for the red-light district in Adelaide taxicab lingo at 2 am because that's where we were deposited.

We aimlessly wandered the streets of this downtrodden area and our perception of the beautiful town of Adelaide was becoming a lot less appealing. Out of desperation, we approached a parked police car with a lone cop who, as it turned out, had been watching us as he realized we were out of our element. "Can I help you fellas?" he quipped in his distinct Australian dialect.

"Yes, we would like to find a place to have breakfast."

"O.K., hop in, I will take you there. You may have noticed this is not an area to find a diner" he added.

When we got into the car, I began to think he was going to run us in and book us for loitering. I never heard of a cop who would take you to a place to eat, especially in the wee small hours. He not only did that but came in and had breakfast with us.

Musings on a Musical Journey

That was the start of a week-long friendship. He became our Adelaide tour guide for the week with trips to the marvelous Australian wine country, dinners with him and his fiancé, and an invite to his mother's house who was a fabulous artist. The time in Adelaide was one of my all-time favorite tour stops because of the fabulous people we met as well as the beautiful concert hall that we performed in.

The trip to Perth was an exceptional stop in that it is one of the world's most remote cities. Located on the west coast of the continent it had the feeling of being a world onto itself. We were told that it was one of the best places to live on the planet.

Arriving at the hotel and waiting for our rooms to be ready for occupancy I noticed an interesting sculpture in a rotunda. It caught my attention and I decided to give it a closer look. As I approached, I noticed a plaque affixed to the base. The inscription read "Gift of Benita Mussolini." "Wow," I thought, "Could that be who I think it is?" The maître d'hôtel assured me that she was indeed the daughter of the infamous Benito Mussolini, the former Prime Minister of Italy.

When World War II was nearing an end she disowned her father and moved to Perth to be as far away from the rest of the world as possible. Upon her arrival, she became one of Australia's leading arts patrons and philanthropists to lend a semblance of decency to the family legacy.

In my fifty years of working in New York, I went on a total of 39 tours. I suppose that these experiences coupled with the early days on the road with the big bands qualify me as an official New York City *Road Rat*. How I ever got back home in one piece is hard to fathom.

Chapter 9
My Visit to North Korea, February 2008

I suppose that I am one of the few that most people know who went to North Korea and came back to tell the story. In 2008, I was a member of the New York Philharmonic invited to Pyongyang in North Korea to play for the elite hard-core comrades and followers of Kim Jong-il. We were to fly to Beijing, China (15 hours of flight) to spend just one day there for clearance before going on to Pyongyang, North Korea. There, we would play one concert and then return to New York two days later.

Due to the unknowns of what to expect, there was downright fear on the part of the orchestra. Many years of threats against the West by the suspicious leader of North Korea caused much anxiety. We were assured however that a "softening" on the part of leader Kim Jong-il would guarantee our safe return. My wife was especially worried due to everything we had read and heard about the notorious leader of North Korea, but we both realized that this would be the opportunity of a lifetime. Also, we surmised, what is the danger when you are traveling with such a large, world-renowned orchestra? On the other hand, who really knew what leader Kim had in store for us.

When we arrived in Beijing, we had a briefing in the ballroom of the Grand Hyatt Regency where we were to stay

Musings on a Musical Journey

overnight before departing on a charter flight to Pyongyang. The briefing was given by the President of the Philharmonic Zarin Mehta, plus a woman from the Swedish Embassy in North Korea. Because the United States did not, at that time, have relations with North Korea and we were technically considered to still be at war with that country, there was no United States Embassy there. Most of the information given at that briefing was useful, but also very alarming. The silence in the room was testament to the underlying fear that we all felt.

We were told in our briefing, for example, that many of the Anti-American propaganda posters that had adorned the city were to be taken down before our arrival, but as I will relate later, this would not be the case.

I want to add a commentary about Beijing; it was an entirely different city than I remembered from twenty years before when I last visited with the New York Philharmonic. In 1988, my impression of the city was a confused mess, saturated with poor downtrodden people on bicycles and many ugly or non-descript buildings. Worst of all had been the pollution that descended dark and heavy on everyone and everything. Now, I saw new construction everywhere and it was so much more esthetically pleasing than what I had seen on my prior trip.

In contrast to my earlier visit, there were large numbers of late model, luxury automobiles on traffic-congested streets. This may have been because of the upcoming Olympic Games. Interesting to see how the strong influence of Capitalism, so apparent on this visit, seems to have changed the living situation dramatically, in a country that still clings to Totalitarianism. What a contrast I would find when I arrived in North Korea.

Another surprise came when our cell phones were confiscated before we exited the charter plane. We were told

Saxophone Troubadour

that these would be returned to us on our flight back to Seoul two days later. It seems that only Kim Jong-il and his top-ranking officials had access to cellphones and the internet. It was a common belief among Americans that Kim Jong-il was highly proficient in computer and electronic functions. How arrogant is that?

For security reasons, we flew a circuitous route from China to Pyongyang. I never found out why or for whom the security was needed. Flying due east from Beijing to Pyongyang would have saved a considerable amount of time and fuel, rather than the route we took north along the coast of mainland China, up and over Manchuria and then south over North Korea. We were told in our briefing that we would be the first group since the beginning of the Korean War to fly directly into the forbidden airspace, over the Yellow Sea into the Korean peninsula. Someone in authority apparently decided, at the last minute, to forbid it again; hence, the detour.

North Korea is pretty *INTENSE*. Upon landing at the airport, my first thought was that we had taken a wrong turn and landed on another planet. My original misgivings about going on this trip came rushing back to me—how could participating in music for an elite audience of communists do anything to help the poor starving people in this country?

During the bus ride from the airport, we were shocked at the sight of huge billboards that depicted a Korean soldier piercing the hearts of two American GIs with a giant bayonet as well as another of a gigantic fist coming down on the head of an American soldier in a foxhole. Still other signs encouraged the people to be brave and to resist the *Evil Empire* of the United States. It is apparent that, for diplomatic reasons, these posters were not shown in the PBS Concert/ Documentary that aired after our return.

Musings on a Musical Journey

Pyongyang is the showplace of North Korea. It is the place where the North Korean elite would like the rest of the world to believe is representative of their entire country, but it seemed to me that it is not. Additionally, the city presents a veneer of modern life, but a look behind the scenes shows the poverty and want that we all anticipated. Glitzy lights await the traveler upon entry into the city, but we later learned that these lights are turned off when the visitors leave the area. Most residents don't have enough electricity to light their living spaces, and many don't have any light at all.

It is an eerie sight to pass a huge apartment complex and to note that most of it is in complete darkness. I assume that when the government decides to showcase the city lights, the residents have to turn out their home lights. I met a foreign news correspondent for CBS who told me that when he arrived in Pyongyang a few days prior, none of the elaborate lighting was on in the downtown area. He told of a certain writer whose description of Pyongyang at night was a black page.

Huge roadways with NO CARS on them really left an impression. The overwhelming percentage of the population traveled by foot, regardless of weather and distance. People in the streets did not look poor, but few of them were riding the existing buses. Rush hour in Pyongyang consists of throngs of people waiting for a bus, but even longer lines of people walking in silent, orderly lines. In all my years of working and living in New York City, where crowds are plentiful and bus lines are long and full of impatient commuters, I never saw a crowd of bunched together people to even remotely compare. I didn't notice any railroads or even gas stations along the thoroughfare. Sidewalks are teeming while wide boulevards and mammoth bridges are

Saxophone Troubadour

empty of vehicles. The good news is that the people looked physically healthy and there was little pollution.

I could only surmise that these huge thoroughfares were designed for military displays, of which there were said to be many. In 2008, they made no secret of the fact that the U.S. and Japan are their mortal enemies and they warn that the entire population must be ever alert. The constant huge displays of force as shown on U.S. television and North Korean print highlighted their vast military equipment with all the Pyongyang residents in attendance (voluntarily? I think not). The bookstore in our hotel lobby contained a heavy supply of propaganda along with DVDs of the many military functions that happen in the city. Mammoth displays of tanks, rockets, and various military equipment were, for us, pretty scary stuff!

Shortly after arriving in Pyongyang, we were taken by bus to see and hear a fantastic concert of dance, singing, and instrumental music by the Pyongyang Performing Arts Troupe. The show was somewhat reminiscent of a Radio City Music Hall presentation with all of the slick lighting, colorful costumes, over-the-top choreography, technical wizardry and impeccably flawless performances from all involved.

The coordination and precision was slicker than anything I could have ever imagined. Their standards of performance are exceedingly high. I supposed that if any of the performers or workers had the audacity to miss a cue, they would have been relieved of their position and moved to another town. We were told that the privilege of living in Pyongyang was by invitation only, and that residents are typically moved from the *showcase city* after their usefulness was no longer apparent.

Unbelievable banquets were prepared for us, consisting of a variety of meat and seafood delicacies. Exquisite

Musings on a Musical Journey

pastries and desserts topped off fabulous feasts. Hard to digest these incredibly wonderful feasts when thinking of the vast number of people who were starving in the rest of the country. I couldn't help remembering the masses that we observed who were working in snow covered fields to plant food with yak drawn plows.

The next morning, we were divided into groups and assigned our own *Minders*. These were government officials whose function was (supposedly) to keep us informed. Our particular group was about ten people. Out minder was a person who was educated at Yale University and gave every appearance of being an ordinary forty-year-old American businessman. His English was clear and articulate and he possessed an elegant charm. It seemed apparent, however, that his main function was to monitor our activities. When I asked him why North Koreans do not like jazz, he quickly responded that jazz just doesn't appeal to the people. It was obvious to me that since jazz is an individual form of expression, the government wanted the people to respond only to subjects that glorified the government as a collective.

Our own concert day began with a 9:30 am to 12 noon rehearsal, in concert dress (not typical for our rehearsals in the States), that was attended by many students and journalists. This event was also used as an opportunity to present gifts to the attending students as well as to cover any mishaps that might happen in the live TV performance scheduled for that evening. As the rehearsal progressed, everyone in attendance and the orchestra became more relaxed. The musicians seemed to have found their niche and the music flowed effortlessly. We found, however, that it was difficult to get the North Koreans to show excitement about anything; it was obvious that they are not permitted to exchange conversation with the *outsiders*. When I saw

Saxophone Troubadour

some of the North Korean musicians backstage who had performed for us the previous evening, I observed that they smiled from a distance, but quickly walked away when I approached with an outstretched hand.

At the 6:30 pm evening performance, the place was packed with a very orderly, well mannered, dignified audience. They were exquisitely and colorfully dressed men and women who appeared to have been outfitted by the same Fifth Avenue tailor. The one thing that they all had in common was an official red button with a likeness of Kim Jong-il that they wore prominently on their clothing. We later learned that failure to wear the pin is considered to be highly disrespectful to the leader. In North Korea, disrespect for the leader can have dire consequences.

Because I was not on stage for the first two pieces, Wagner's "Prelude to the Act III of Lohengrin" and Dvorak's Symphony no. 9 "From the New World", I watched from the TV monitors backstage. Even from that view, it was apparent that the audience was not prepared to show an excess of emotion. It seemed to me that we had come upon a group of Stepford wives and husbands. Before beginning the third piece, George Gershwin's "American in Paris", Maestro Loren Maazel gave a brief talk on the composer and the music. He concluded by saying that "Perhaps the day will come when a composer will write a work entitled 'An American in Pyongyang'". The audience erupted into rapturous applause that rattled the rafters. This was the first sign that showed the people to have human traits, though definitely programmed.

At that time, I had played the Gershwin "American in Paris" for over 45 years and I could not remember a performance such as this one. The beginning of the piece is one of the most exciting, enthusiastic and joyful starts of any music ever written. It is, to me, a display of distinct

Musings on a Musical Journey

Americana. Since the saxophone part doesn't start until several minutes into the piece, I always enjoy watching the smiling and happy faces of the audience. There's nothing like the taxi horns that occur in the opening and closing sections of the work to get the attention of the audience. This time, it was serious faces that looked straight ahead with little to no reaction. My interpretation of this behavior was that, because jazz music is forbidden (really!!) in North Korea, it would not be a good thing for a rank-and-file person to get caught on camera with a look of enjoyment. The next two pieces on the program, Bernstein's "Candide" and Bizet's "Farandole from L'Arlesienne Suite No. 2", seemed to move the audience a little more.

The final work was a gorgeous arrangement of a piece entitled "Arirang", which is a national folk song of both North and South Korea. This occasion was my first introduction to this distinctly Korean tune. This performance literally brought tears to the eyes of many men and women. There was no holding back the emotions that filled the room at this point. I would equate this to an American's reaction to the playing of "America the Beautiful." I couldn't help but think that if this entire group of people were programmed to react only as they did, they surely all deserved Oscars.

The final applause at the end of the concert lasted for quite a while after the orchestra left the stage. Many of the orchestra members returned to the stage while the applause continued unabated, accompanied by hands waving back and forth. The tears in the eyes of most of the audience at this point was reason enough to make the trip worthwhile, as we saw two diverse cultures come together in unified appreciation of the performance. It made a lasting impression on me as I saw the unification of both North and South (orchestra members present) Koreans.

Saxophone Troubadour

The eighteen-hour trip back home aboard Asiana Airlines didn't feel so bad or even long. It was a relief to leave North Korea and return to the modern hustle and bustle of our *real world* as we entered Seoul, South Korea. It was even greater to be going home. My thoughts lingered on the power of music and how it is very much like a hug....it doesn't deceive. If our music got through to only one person, it made everything worthwhile. I really believe that eventually North Korea will wake up and join the prosperity of other nations. I kept thinking that our concert in North Korea ignited a small, but very significant spark.

On the final leg of the trip, I pondered the wonders and good fortune that we have as Americans. I was choked up while humming "America the Beautiful" to myself.

Musings on a Musical Journey

Chapter 10
Some Special Recollections

My best friend George

There are many personal acquaintances that I fondly remember in my fifty-five years of activity in the music business. Aside from the many fabulous musical talents that crossed my path, there were several who demonstrated excellent personal relations even in this highly competitive work. This business could be very tough and at times cruel. As in any field, everyone needs a friend.

I was most fortunate to have become friends with a wonderful musician, George Marge, not long after I began college at the Eastman School of Music in 1954. George was two years ahead of me in school so there were several years that our paths did not cross after our graduations.

We had not been in touch with each other for five years until a chance meeting on West 50th Street and Sixth Avenue in New York City. George was working at Radio City Music Hall and was on a three-hour break between shows. After a brief chat, he invited me to his apartment to meet his wife Joanna. Little did I realize at the time, but it was during that short period that my life was about to change.

Meeting Joanna was wonderful. I hadn't been in their quaint West 55th Street apartment more than a few minutes when they both made me feel comfortably welcome. George was always a great conversationalist and this meeting was no exception. He asked what my plans were after my discharge from the army. When I told him that I was all set to move to Oakland, California to attend Mills College for a master's degree in music composition a look of dismay quickly came across his face.

I related my interest in composing and having the opportunity to study with the legendary Darius Milhaud, which I considered to be a great honor. George's response to this set me back and was the beginning of a whole new direction to my future.

George could be very persuasive. His Lebanese heritage provided him with a set of big brown intense eyes that could mesmerize you. The radiance of his smile displayed the genuine warmth of his being. He remarked, "What on Earth are you going to Oakland, California for? New York is the place, and why do you want to go all that way to study composition?" he retorted.

George was always one to give good advice and as much as this had me reeling, it made much sense. George continued, "You are a good instrumentalist. Why not come to New York and get your feet wet in the music business and get a master's degree here in the big city? If the city doesn't agree with you, then you can go to another location and be a composer."

He was adamant in his advice and when George needed to make a point, he could be most convincing. George's penetrating look and forthcoming nature showed up in his intense look which was always straight into one's eyes. In any case, it was well worth considering. And since I was free the following day, I decided to take a trip to East 104th Street to take a look at the Manhattan School of Music.

The Manhattan School in 1960 was a converted brownstone that was originally the Union Settlement

Musings on a Musical Journey

Association and located in an East Harlem residential neighborhood. It was much like entering a privately owned mansion and unlike any place that I could ever imagine to be a college. Upon entering, a feeling of warmth pervaded the building, and I was immediately attracted to the ambiance and artistic environment. I had not been there very long when I was introduced to Nicolas Flagello the eminent professor of composition. After checking into my resumé he suggested that I apply to the school as a clarinet major with a minor in composition. The practicality of the whole process made much sense and I immediately thought, George knows what he's talking about.

This is exactly where I need to be! It was during that period that George and I became best friends. He was not only like a brother, but he became my very influential mentor. Whenever I needed guidance George was on the spot and was never wrong with his advice.

In a matter of a few short years, George rose to the top of his game. He would practice and study incessantly and became a great influence on me in that respect. His hard work was never at the expense of his family, however, as he would always make sure that business did not get in the way of his home life.

George also understood and valued real friendship. He would call frequently to check on my latest activities or often just to chew the fat. He even went so far as to reprimand me for not calling him. I can still hear him giving it to me over the phone, "I'm always calling, why don't you give me a call once in a while?" he would remark. "That's what friends do!"

George was a shrewd businessman, but he was never deceptive. As far as I knew he did not have a degree from a business school, but he knew the ins and outs thoroughly. His ability to remember names and faces was uncanny. As

Saxophone Troubadour

a result, he was very well-liked and respected for the sincere humanness he exuded as well as for his outstanding musical abilities. These traits led him to become the top choice on the majority of contractors' lists in NY.

His brotherly traits even included reminding me to keep in touch with doctors and dentists. I would be so obsessive about my music development that I would often neglect important health matters. George could be somewhat nagging at times, but his genuine concern would always manage to get through to me and as usual, he was right.

I never knew anyone who could cover as many bases as George. From 1963 to 1985 he seemed to have been on every recording date that took place in New York. His colleagues nicknamed him *Dates*. He was in so many places that the description of his activities was, *Two-thirds of the world is covered in water; the other one-third is covered by George Marge*. I was certain that he had a clone.

George had an incessant thirst for improving on all of his many instruments. He would work on sound production for the variety of styles that he was called upon to perform. From a symphonic tone quality on an oboe to a raucous rock and roll baritone sax and beyond, he could simulate the exact sound that music makers needed for their varied products.

Since his main thing was playing on recording sessions, he made absolutely sure that every sound was right for the microphone. Saxophones needed to be full and non-buzzing, flute sounds were clear and non-airy, clarinets were mellow and dark, qualities that could be adjusted for the many different styles he was asked to duplicate.

He also played a variety of recorders and ocarinas that were specialty sounds needed mostly for children's or comedic music. Primarily, George was always looking for

Musings on a Musical Journey

ways to be helpful, a trait that was a carryover into his everyday life. I always felt that George's biggest draw was his ever-present determination to deliver a product that was right for whatever project he undertook.

George knew how to deal with every situation, good and bad. He was always on top of any given moment. A personal recollection that he guided me through was on a particular one-hour commercial jingle date. Jingle dates were recordings for TV/radio ads that were usually set for one-to-three-hour time slots. They were also scheduled so that there would be provisions for overtime in the event of unforeseen problems. The possible overtime periods could be anywhere from twenty to forty minutes.

The referenced date was ordered for a 10 to 11 am Monday with a possible twenty-minute overtime. It was booked a week ahead since it was using a large orchestra with a big string section. The Sunday evening prior, at approximately 10 pm, the phone rang with a call for a different jingle at 9 am to 10 am, with a possible forty-minute overtime.

It was for a very busy office where I did quite a lot of work and was not disposed to turning down. Since it was late and with not much wiggle-room I asked who else was called for both dates.

The other woodwind was the busiest woodwind player of the day, Phil Bodner. Since I knew him to be a seasoned pro, I decided to phone him to see how he would be handling this. After a brief discussion, we agreed that Warner/Levinson the company for the 9 am scheduled date was very efficient in their timing and was not inclined to use overtime. I was a little leery but was willing to go ahead if the older and wiser Phil thought that it would work out.

Upon arriving at the studio situated on the fifth floor of the Ed Sullivan Theater building on 53rd Street and

Saxophone Troubadour

Broadway, I was quite relieved to see that the music was a simple little ditty. *Great*, I thought, *We should be out of here in less than half an hour.*

Added to that was the fact that 777 Seventh Avenue, a prominent studio during that period, was a stone's throw away. I breathed a sigh of relief since that was where the 10 am date was to take place.

Forty minutes later my blood pressure started going up when it was decided that the music we were slated to record was not suitable for the product, in the producer's estimation. 10 am came and we had not recorded a single usable tune and now my heart was doing a jittery dance. Phil on the other hand, was as cool as a cucumber, peering straight ahead and not muttering a word.

At 10:40 am, by some strange miracle, we managed to finish the recording to everyone's satisfaction. I beat it out of the place, quickly packing my instrument and doing an Olympic-style sprint. Phil seemed to be sauntering along but arrived at the 777 studio just as I did. We both entered to a hushed sound of a sixty-piece orchestra. The silence was deafening until the thundering voice of the conductor boomed "I know Phil, but who the F—K are you?!"

At that point, I was well past the jittery heart dance and ready to wither away. The orchestra, made up mostly of a string section consisting of New York City ringers, were frozen in their seats. Trudging to my seat felt like I was on the last walk to the electric chair.

I was about to get down on my knees, kiss the conductor's feet and plead for forgiveness when good ole' George whispered, while swabbing his oboe, "Shut up, don't say a word, take out your clarinet and make like nothing happened." So as usual I listened to George.

The music we were about to record was the opening to Beethoven's *Fifth Symphony*, a very familiar four-note motif. Since the whole score was only three minutes, we were able to record it to everyone's satisfaction in one take. The session was miraculously declared done and when I looked at the clock it was 10:59 am...... WHEW!!

I was about to rush up to the podium and profusely apologize to the conductor when George again whispered, while packing his instrument, "Shut up! Pack up and get out of here fast."

"But George, I have to say something."

"Just leave, because this man is pretty angry and if you get within ten feet of him you don't know what he might do. JUST LEAVE!" was Georges' final statement.

Again, I listened to George and again he was right. Two weeks later I was called by the same office and the same conductor to do another recording session. As stated, he didn't know me, and he still didn't.

That was all right with me because I didn't care what he called me as long as he called me to do his dates. So, George's mentoring, professional understanding, and wisdom bailed me out of a situation that could have had disastrous consequences. Another lesson in Business 101 that my buddy taught me, on the job.

George tragically passed away on August 22, 1985, at the age of 52. The shock was unbelievably devastating. Here was a person so full of life and suddenly he was gone. I had planned a visit to see him on that afternoon when I received a call from his wife Joanna. She delivered the agonizing news that he had passed away during that early Thursday morning while at the River Edge, New Jersey hospital emergency room. I had just spoken to him a few hours earlier.

The Great Conductor must have needed a first call recording artist because He called the best, my best friend George.

Saxophone Troubadour

A Night at the Opera, 1987

Woody Allen's comment that "80 percent of success is showing up" has several meanings. Listening and participation are necessities but, in my case, it was simply physically "showing up."

Logistics are sometimes more difficult than the actual job itself. Being in the right place on the right date, on time, with the right instrument(s), proper attire and correct attitude are essentials to getting the job done. As conscientious as one can be, however, there are sometimes setbacks for a variety of reasons.

Keeping accurate and legible date books was always a challenge for me particularly at the start of each new year. December of 1987 was a specific case in point since it included performances of three short one-act operas at the Met.

They were *Parade* by Eric Satie, *Dialogues des Carmélites* by Francois Poulenc, and *L'Enfant et les Sortileges* by Maurice Ravel. My job as E-flat Clarinetist was to play in *Parade* and *L'Enfant et les Sortileges* with a 45-minute break during *Dialogues* since there was no E-flat Clarinet part involved in that work.

The evening started innocently as I showed up at my regular job, *Cats*, at the Winter Garden Theatre on Broadway and 50th Street. I moseyed into the back-stage band area around 7:40 pm for an 8:00 pm performance startled to find the substitute, Joel Kaye sitting in my chair preparing to play the show. The first thought was that I made a simple mistake in hiring a replacement for the evening since my 1988 date book did not show that I was to be off. Luckily, I also had my 1987 date book handy and when I opened it to my 1987 calendar, shock riddled my body as if I had been hit by a lightning bolt. There in big

Musings on a Musical Journey

bold print was MET 8:00 pm! Because I had already started to use my 1988 book in December, it was now apparent that I had neglected to transfer the date from my 1987 book.

Tearing across the backstage area, recklessly darting in and out of props and actors dressed as felines, while carrying a flute, piccolo, and tenor sax I arrived at the stage door. Here I borrowed a load of nickels and dimes from the stage door manager while getting him to hold my flute, piccolo, and tenor sax so I could insert coins into the pay phone. This was 1987 after all, still several years before we all had cell phones.

I was able to reach Bob Sirinek, the Met Opera orchestra manager, a few minutes before 8:00 pm and nervously told him in a freaked-out voice that I was not going to get there for the 8:00 pm start. Since I was far from relaxed, the met manager thought I was injured. "Please tell Roger Hillyer the principal clarinetist to cover my part in the first opera, *Parade*." I extorted. Although Roger was the principal E-flat clarinetist, at this performance he was playing the solo Bb Clarinet part and didn't even have his E-flat instrument at the Met.

"Are you O.K.?" Bob implored. "I'm fine! Just get the word to Roger" I answered. "But what happened?" Bob insisted. "Please, Bob, get the word to Roger" I replied in a tense voice. "But what happened?", Bob repeated. To save time and avoid a lengthy explanation I blurted out "My car broke down" and quickly hung up.

Because start of show-time had passed I had no trouble getting a cab right outside the stage door on 7th Ave and 50th Street My tux and E-flat clarinet were fortunately at West 80th Street and Broadway so it was a quick ride uptown. I relaxed a little knowing there was no way I was ever going to get to the Met before the end of the first opera.

Saxophone Troubadour

I had the taxi wait for me at the corner of West 80th Street and Broadway while I went upstairs to get my instrument and tuxedo. Even though there was no need to hurry at this point I was hoping to arrive at the Met orchestra locker room before the end of the first opera. My hope was to find a quiet corner where I could avoid seeing much of the orchestra especially the personnel manager. I wanted to concentrate on my impending music performance and not have to spend time explaining the embarrassing situation.

My timing could not have been worse since the first person I ran into was the conductor Manual Rosenthal who was just exiting the orchestra pit at the completion of the first opera.

Mssr. Rosenthal was a well-known musical personality in both France and the U.S. He was a former student and a personal friend of the composer Maurice Ravel and was highly respected around the world for his skills as a conductor. He was also a delightful and friendly human being. His warmth came through with dignified grace.

When he saw me, his face lit up and he raced over, extending an embrace, and exclaimed, "Monsieur, are you all right? I understand you had a car accident," he continued. Not knowing how to respond I simply thanked him and expressed my regrets at any confusion I could have caused. He assured me that everything turned out fine and there was no need for concern.

The rest of the evening was routine in that the performance was good without any uncommon problems. The only problems were in explaining to several concerned colleagues that I was doing fine, my car was in good operation, calming my nerves and that I was in no need of help in getting a ride home. Of course, thanking Roger

Musings on a Musical Journey

Hillyer was of most importance because he had my back and covered the part so that I was hardly missed.

Big Band Days of the 1960s and 1980s

The main big-band era occurred from the 1930s through the 1950s. There were many swing bands primarily in the United States and England that thrived in the years before, during, and following World War II. During the 1950s the times were changing with the advent of television and the slow demise of ballroom dance halls began. By the 1960s the big bands were all but dissolved, except for a few better well-known carryover bands such as Benny Goodman, Count Basie, Duke Ellington, Glenn Miller, Tommy and Jimmy Dorsey, and Woody Herman, all of which continued after the deaths of their leaders. Music tastes in general were moving away from the *Great American Songbook* to Rock and Roll.

The first job that I was offered after finishing a master's degree at the Manhattan School of Music was as a tenor sax player with the Tommy Dorsey band led by Warren Covington. It was a four-month tour of the United States playing at several state fairs.

I was not thrilled at having to leave my wife Charlotte alone during a summer in New York but the prospect of making a fairly decent paycheck during that period was a necessity. Getting back on our feet after my spending a year completing school left us financially precarious.

The engagement consisted of a staged review by the band with featured soloists Les Paul, Mary Ford, and Jimmy Dean. We were scheduled to play one-week periods throughout the Midwest and the Eastern United States. We would travel on Mondays and play two one-hour shows daily in each state. The circuit consisted of Michigan, Ohio, Illinois, Iowa, Indiana, Wisconsin, Kansas, Kentucky, West

Saxophone Troubadour

Virginia, Virginia, North Carolina, and South Carolina. It was quite an extensive trip for my first experience with a big band.

The downside of the tour was that we were required to find our own living accommodations in each town where we played. This meant that traveling had to be done on our day off, but finding a suitable room to live in was required. Until we got used to the routine some of our living conditions were less than desirable. Staying at low-grade hotels or even at YMCAs got to be a bit trying. We found after a couple of weeks of misery, conducting some local research was necessary. We discovered that there were rooms for rent available in private homes in most of the areas. We would make plans the week previous to each stop and this proved to be a solution to the living situations.

In Lawrence, Kansas one of my band colleagues and I hit the jackpot by contacting an elderly woman who had an incredibly huge Victorian-style house close to our venue. The woman was the retired professor of piano at the University of Kansas and a thoroughly wonderful person. Her home was beautifully decorated with large rooms and a separate studio room that contained twin nine-foot Bechstein grand pianos. We also had separate large bedrooms at a very low rental, which was more than we could have wished for. That was a week that we wished could have lasted for the entire summer.

Because we were doing state fairs our jobs were outdoors in make-shift stage settings which were not really weatherproof. Most of the time the performance coverings were sufficient but on a couple of bad storm experiences, it got a bit touch-and-go. Les Paul's electronic equipment was not suited to any kind of water exposure and when it happened on a couple of occasions the electric sparks were flying, and Les could be heard over the rumbling thunder

Musings on a Musical Journey

using every four-letter word invented. As uncomfortably soaked as the band got, we still managed to find the situation humorous.

A band that I particularly enjoyed playing with was Richard Maltby's. Richard was a talented arranger whose work covered a wide range from radio, recordings, and specialty work for notable singers Vic Damone, Sarah Vaughn, Peggy Lee, and Ethel Merman to serving as conductor/writer for Lawrence Welk. He not only was a seasoned pro but a kind gentleman who was a pleasure to work for. His big hit was the theme from the movie *The Man with the Golden Arm* which he composed and arranged.

Playing in his band was a joy for me as just about every arrangement had a featured tenor sax solo which allowed me to shine. I remember thinking that I was covering a lot of ground on every three-hour gig, getting up from my chair and traveling to the microphone. The music was always very tastefully written with much space for personal musical exposure.

I sometimes wondered if Mr. Maltby hired me for my musical abilities or my driving. He owned a large size Oldsmobile and he liked to sit in the passenger front seat where he could keep an eye on the speedometer. Since he was a bit of a nervous traveler, he was adamant about not speeding. This was a direct opposite from most road band people who were always racing to get to the next job. Driving 15 miles over the posted speed limit was the usual norm. Richard always commented to me on how safe he felt with my driving. I decided to keep that a priority so that he would call me for his work, regardless of how he felt about my playing.

Probably the best thrill I ever had of playing in a name band was working for Benny Goodman, the King of Swing. What came out of that man's clarinet was pure elegance. It

Saxophone Troubadour

was often difficult to concentrate on playing my part when I would be constantly in awe of his artistry. He was without question the greatest big band instrumentalist that I was honored to have played with, even though his demeanor could often leave much to be desired.

Benny was famous for his signature facial expression that was known as "the ray". When a player didn't perform up to his expectations, he would look over the top of his rimmed glasses with a stare that resembled a laser beam. Before muttering a word, he would let that look penetrate until its vibes were well felt.

I was on the receiving end of such an event when at a rehearsal he abruptly stopped the band to deal me an admonishment for swooping up on the lead-in note to his theme song *Let's Dance*. After a moment of silence which felt like an eternity, he let *the ray* settle in before asking, "Is that the modern style?"

Not understanding the question, I answered, "What do you mean?"

Again, *the ray* lasered across the room before he heatedly replied, "Hit the note on the head, no slurps in this band."

It was one of the best lessons I ever had and regardless of how ungently it was delivered, was one that I never forgot.

A band that was a delight to be a part of was Larry Elgart's. Larry was a marvelous saxophonist whose musical elegance was without peer. Matching his sound took much concentration and discipline. The beautiful tone quality he produced was a study in quiet projection, never forced but always filling the room.

Larry would typically meet the band members on the bus at the start of road trips with a congenial greeting along with a split of whiskey. It was always interesting to sit with him on bus trips and endlessly discuss music and

Musings on a Musical Journey

musicians. I only wished I had more opportunities to work with him. He was a pleasure not only as a musician but even more so as a gentleman. My stints with his band were during the 1970s when road band gigs were on their demise.

Playing with Sammy Kaye's orchestra was not always fun from a musical standpoint because of the stiff commercial nature of the style we needed to play. I enjoyed working with the band mainly because Sammy was a kind sort and honest in his pursuit to satisfy the tastes of the dancers. He made no pretensions as to the nature of his music and as a result, had one of the most successful bands of the dance era. His style required a precise steady beat that was devoid of any rhythmic flexibility. We would describe many of the arrangements as *businessman's bounce*.

A personal high note remembrance happened in 1961 while playing a dance gig with Warren Covington's Band in a hotel ballroom in Des Moines, Iowa. We had a one-hour break in the middle of the affair to accommodate speeches and awards. During the engagement, we learned that Les Brown's "Band of Renown" was playing directly across the street in a beautiful ballroom. Hearing that band live was a treat. The precision, musicality, and fabulous soloists blew me away. I was able to meet a couple of the musicians and was invited to an after-hours jam session at a popular Des Moines jazz club called *The Library*.

The club was packed with people and at the 2 am closing time the fun started. Between Warren Covington's Band and Les Brown's, we must have had twenty musicians with their instruments ready to wail. We all managed to have good "session manners" so that everyone present got a chance to be a soloist. The rhythm section guys had to play straight through since there were no replacements for piano, bass, or drum players. They didn't seem to mind and stayed the whole morning which didn't wrap up until 8 am. It was a night to remember, and I cannot forget going outside to the blazing Mid-west sun in the early morning after having spent the previous eight hours in a darkened room. The drummer from Les Brown's band and I went for breakfast where we talked music and enjoyed the exciting aftermath of a magical night.

Although I did not spend a large part of my career playing with the big bands, they were all wonderful experiences. At times I would wish that I had been born 20 years earlier to have been part of that remarkable era. Once after completing a jazzy clarinet solo my idol Jimmy Abato complimented me by saying, "If you had been born twenty years earlier you would have had your own band." Coming from Jimmy that remark made my heart and head swell.

One of my fondest memories was of playing a gig with Warren Covington's Band in Binghamton, New York in 1962. The engagement was from 9:00PM to 12 Midnight after which my parents invited the entire band of 17 plus Warren to our home in nearby Johnson City. My Mother, Anna, loved putting on an Italian feast for large parties at any hour of the day or night. True to her Calabrese heritage she pulled out all the stops and fed a ravenous bunch of musicians a feast that lasted well into the early morning hours. It turned out to be the highlight of the tour as well as for my mom and dad.

We all yearn for good things from our past lives, but I must say that I do very much miss the big bands.

Twin Peaks *Dance of the Dream Man*
In the early 1990s, I had been contracted by Angelo Badalamenti to be a part of David Lynch's new TV show

Musings on a Musical Journey

Twin Peaks. The show was a surprise to many of us because it not only gained success early on but gathered momentum and became a bona fide hit for several seasons on national television's ABC. It was recorded mostly at Excalibur Studio on Eighth Avenue with the excellent Artie Polhemus, recording engineer.

Much of the incidental music and background effect music was improvised with a limited description of what effects were needed. In the original recordings, the woodwind improvisations were performed by Eddie Daniels, Andre Badalamenti, and me. The music was created in many instances with Angelo standing in front of us; his arm movements and facial gestures were all that we had.

At a recording date that occurred early on in the series, I was hired to play tenor sax and clarinet. Upon arriving thirty minutes before the actual start time, I was alone in the studio and proceeded to warm up on the tenor sax in the style of the music I thought would be representative of what would be needed. Mr. Polhemus was mixing a bass line in the control room that was coming through into the studio. It was a sort of minor blues that was very tempting to play along with.

I hadn't played more than a minute or so when David Lynch tore into the room with a look of excitement. I was afraid that my playing was interfering with the mixing that was in progress and would be told to stop. Instead, he harkened me to continue playing and that he wanted to record it. Nothing was written down and at a given cue I just proceeded to improvise off of the aforementioned bass line.

I was surprised that after about twenty choruses of what I thought was beginning to sound tedious Mr. Lynch gave me the cue to wrap it up. It was puzzling for me to think that this undertaking would be of any use to the show, but after witnessing David Lynch's expression I could see that he had something in mind. I asked, "What will you be using this for?"

His reply was "I don't know but I will use it."

David Lynch's talent for knowing what *works* is a key glimpse into the extraordinary vision he has for filmmaking. After recording the music, I could not feel anything of artistic value through the music, but after seeing and hearing the way he used it, it made perfect sense. I suppose it was one of those spur-of-the-moment accidental successes.

I was disappointed that I was not given more credit for creating the tune that was not only used in a featured spot but also permeated through the entire series as a frequent underscore.

Audiences and critics saw the value in David's creation as the music from the show went on to win a gold record and Grammy recognition.

David Gilbert and the Joking Monk

The New York Philharmonic honored my good friend David Gilbert some years ago for winning first prize in their conducting competition. Among the several awards he received was a conducting debut with the orchestra for a one-week engagement consisting of four concerts, along with the assistant conductorship of the orchestra for the entire season.

To celebrate his opening night concert, a group of his friends, including me, took Dave out to a now-defunct watering hole called the *Monk's Inn*, which at the time was located on West 64th Street very near Lincoln Center. The *Monk's Inn* was a cozy place designed for late-night fare and after concert socializing.

Musings on a Musical Journey

The waiters at the restaurant were very slick jesters, often actors who were equipped with many quick one-liners and wonderful witticisms while being appropriately garbed in authentic Monk's robes.

During the evening, our particular waiter kept us constantly amused with some very comedic bantering. After he directed a good-natured jest at Dave's expense, I interjected by saying, "Sir, please treat this gentleman with some respect, after all, he's the new Assistant Conductor of the New York Philharmonic."

"Is that so?" replied the bemused monk, who promptly picked up a butter knife and chimed a water glass. "Can you tell me what note I just hit?" asked the smiling waiter. "No, I'm afraid I cannot," said Dave in a rather astonished voice.

"Well, that explains why you're the Assistant!" said the Monk, as he triumphantly strolled off.

Nunzio *Toots* Mondello

Nunzio *Toots* Mondello was a saxophone innovator, great musician, first-class gentleman, and a man that I considered to be a powerful personal influence. I thought of him as a father figure and role model extraordinaire as well.

During the golden years of the New York studio days, Toots was the model lead alto sax player that the top players of the day would imitate stylistically and technically. The legendary virtuoso Jimmy Abato's famous quote was "Toots wrote the book on American saxophone playing that we all followed."

His warm, lush and energetic quality was a contrast to the bright vibrant sound of the French style that was the former model. His playing evolved from his experience in the swing era of Benny Goodman; it both fit the tastes of

Saxophone Troubadour

big band playing of the day and satisfied the classical tastes of former generations. Toots was the studio man's idol. His influence and spirited drive in the sax section added to Benny's artistry and the Goodman's swing band popularity. His saxophone solo on the original theme song recording of "Let's Dance" is a timeless piece of playing that remains a model of saxophone artistry.

When I arrived on the New York scene in the early 1960s Mr. Mondello was the lead saxophonist for the Ed Sullivan Show, a position he held for the entire 16-year run of that famous television show. He was also on the staff of the CBS network orchestra and a favorite of Jackie Gleason. In addition to being the saxophone soloist on Gleason's *Velvet Brass* recording album, Toots was hailed as the founder of the Royal Order of Raccoons, comedy sketches on the popular Honeymooners (TV Series mid-1950s), and he was literally the toast of the town.

Toots' thirst for musical excellence included classical study. He became a student and close friend to the American composer, Paul Creston. His compositions involved a wide spectrum of materials for numerous instrumental combinations.

I was fortunate to have performed his concertino for saxophone and chamber ensemble on several occasions. His *Soliloquy* for solo flute and *Poem for Flute and Harp,* are favorites throughout the United States and Internationally.

As Mr. Mondello aged and modern styles evolved throughout the broadcast network world, he found it harder to find employment. In the era of waning big band popularity and the ending of many popular TV musical shows such as Jackie Gleason and Ed Sullivan, he went from the first call to very few calls. Unfortunately, during the 1960s and 1970s, his only financial supplement was from social security since musician's royalties and pensions were still not developed. Consequently, he was forced to become financially prudent and to maintain a lifestyle that was far below what he experienced in his heyday.

A favorite New York restaurant, Fontana di Trevi on West 57th Street, across from Carnegie Hall, was a regular haunt of Toots. He was given first-class treatment there even up to the time when he could no longer afford to dine there as regularly as he once did. The management thought highly of him and would even sometimes not charge him for meals. He was touched to the point of tears when during his last days they would deliver food to his West 46th Street apartment free of charge. To the owners of Fontana di Trevi, Toots was a New York legend who often dined regularly there with the likes of Sir Rudolf Bing the general Manager of New York's Metropolitan Opera and Jackie Gleason.

From his earliest days to his last, Toots remained loyal to the Boston Red Sox. He once recalled to me that when he was a young boy his father, who worked at Boston's Fenway Park, took him to meet and shake hands with Babe Ruth. He loved to mimic Ruth's deep voice saying, "Hello son."

During the last two years of his life, Toots was constantly watching mostly sports on a small screen black and white TV while maneuvering rabbit ear antennas. Joe Rabbai, Mitch Weiss, and I decided that since Toots had spent most of his professional life playing on national TV that he should be able to have the luxury of a decent set-up. The three of us chipped in, knowing that he could not afford to buy one for himself, and got him a good-sized set along with a cable subscription. It was one of the most touching moments to watch the tears well up in Toots' eyes when he tuned in and saw it for the first time. The three of us were huge Mondello fans and felt a sense of accomplishment at being able to bring some pleasure to this distinguished, humble gentleman.

Saxophone Troubadour

Toots passed away on November 14, 1992, and died with the same graceful dignity with which he lived. On Saturday, November 13, 1992, Ray Shanfield, Benny Aronoff, and I, who were playing the Broadway show "Cats" at the time, went to visit Toots at Lenox Hill Hospital. We were between shows on a Saturday matinee day and decided to visit him. It was not a pleasant sight to see him since he was near death and barely able to communicate. At one point he managed to open his eyes and with a faint smile said, "It's been a pleasure knowing you guys."

A short while later he passed away.

Since Nunzio Mondello's only surviving family was a second cousin who lived in the Boston area, no plans had been made for a New York funeral or even a memorial service. Joe Rabbai, Mitch Weiss and I again acted and contacted St. Malachy's church. This was referred to as the Broadway Actor's Roman Catholic Church and Toots was a faithful member. When I called the pastor to request a mass, he was most cooperative.

In less than two days of only word-of-mouth communication on the streets of the city the church was overflowing with musicians, actors, and show people, and a touching tribute was given to one of the best-loved and most gracious gentlemen to have been a part of New York, New York.

New York Nightclubs

Two of the most famous nightclubs in New York City after World War II were the Latin Quarter and Copacabana. They rivaled each other as to who brought the best entertainment to Manhattan. During the mid-1960s I worked at the Latin Quarter sporadically and have some nostalgic memories of what New York City once was.

Musings on a Musical Journey

The Latin Quarter was located at the crossroads of Seventh Avenue and Broadway, the north end of Times Square. It was a triangular-shaped three-story building and was well known for the many glittering neon signs on its roof. The most notable of these was the Coca-Cola sign which was one of the most famous of all the Times Square glitz symbols of the day. The LQ was one of the best-known showplaces in the world and would often have crowds until 3 am watching shows, dining, and dancing.

Playing shows at the Copa was a slam-bang affair of segueing through piles of music from a fast and furious opener to various acts which could consist of a dog act, a featured singer, comics, dancers, or more and always closed with a rip-roaring can-can number with scantily clad gorgeous showgirls. Many of the most famous pop entertainers in the world were regularly showcased and our band leader Joe Lombardi would keep things going at a rapid pace.

My most vivid memory was not formed while playing the shows, however; but instead on the two breaks between the 9 pm show and the 11 pm show when I would hurry upstairs to the outdoor roof and plant myself under the Coca-Cola sign where I would practice flute. There I was showered in light from above while blowing my flute, accompanied from below by the cacophonous sound of taxi horns. It gave me a feeling of being the lone overseer of Times Square and is one of the most unusual New York experiences in my memory.

I felt saddened when times changed, the NY nightclub scene became a thing of the past, and many entertainment personalities deserted the city for the West Coast. Such exciting days and numerous vivid recollections of my career were starting to roll. This was the beginning of many years of a journey that I look back on with fond memories.

Saxophone Troubadour

Golden Boy Memories

When Sammy Davis did *Golden Boy* on Broadway, I occasionally subbed for one of the reed players. One night before the show, I was standing out in the alley having a smoke as we all did back then with one of my colleagues, Ray Shanfeld. We were passing the time with small talk and gathering nicotine tar when SD comes sauntering up the walk on his way to the stage door. Sammy was always very friendly in those days and gave a warm hello.

My friend told SD that he had photographs from a recent cast party of *Golden Boy*. Sammy's reply was, "Great man, bring them up to my dressing room when you have a chance."

Ray went downstairs immediately, got the snapshots, and went up to SD's room. My friend's habit of pointing his finger at the person he was addressing did not sit well with Sammy.

When my friend returned to the band room I asked him how SD liked the pictures. He told me that when Sammy opened the door he pointed his finger not far from SD's face and said, "You're going to love these shots." Sammy immediately barked back, "Don't point your finger at me, Mother F****r!" and slammed the door in his face. A few days later SD must have forgotten the whole thing and greeted everyone as if nothing had happened.

One Other More Pleasant Recollection

Not long after *Golden Boy* closed on Broadway it was resurrected and played for eight weeks at the New York State Theater at Lincoln Center in New York. I was hired to play the first reed book in the show, and it turned out to be a very happy, pleasurable gig. The show in many ways was even better than the Broadway run in that the NY State theater was much larger and more accessible to the wonderful staging and overall ambiance of the show's dramatic music and lyrics.

The production lost none of the luster and charm of the original show and was tightened up. The orchestra pit of the NY State theater was designed to seat a full symphony orchestra of 90+ players and was a dream come true for a mere twenty-six-piece Broadway pit band. One of the few times in my 38 years of playing on Broadway that I didn't feel like a sardine with a clarinet in its mouth. It was in many ways the ultimate show gig.

Sammy's musical director and conductor of many years was a wonderful musician and great guy by the name of George Rhodes. He did not conduct the Broadway run but did this one and maintained a high standard and great morale for everyone involved. He was a joy to work with and work for. George was the definitive *true musician and gentleman.*

In about the third week of the run at a Sunday afternoon matinee, I brought my eleven-year-old daughter Marissa with me and had intended for her to wait in the musician's lounge doing her schoolwork while we did the show. Upon running into George backstage, I asked him if he would mind my daughter sitting in the back corner of the orchestra pit. We had plenty of room and various actors, stage people, etc. would often come in and sit back there and not even be noticed.

George, of course, said, "Sure, just make sure she gets a comfortable chair and can see everything."

I got her situated and went to my chair awaiting the start of the show.

The house lights dimmed, George made his entrance, went straight to my daughter, took her hand, and led her directly to the conductor's podium where he had placed a seat right next to his. None of us had any idea of what he had in mind. This guy was the world's greatest mensch. She sat there on cloud nine through the entire show. Talk about star beams coming from an eleven-year-old's eyes.

And when Sammy got wind of this awe-struck kid sitting with the conductor it was as if he played the whole performance for her. On several occasions, he would throw her a kiss, direct lyrics her way, and showed her great affection. Sammy was indeed a ham but he loved kids and went out of his way to make them feel at ease. I often wondered if it was something he missed in his childhood or was it something he remembered with great fondness? Sammy meant it when he sang *Make Someone Happy*.

George and Sammy were good guys.

Saxophone Quartets 1967 – 2014

The delight of my life as a musician has been being a part of and making music with saxophone quartets. The saxophone quartet is the counterpart to the better-known string quartet. String quartets are considered to be the most elite of chamber music ensembles but in my biased opinion sax quartets have a lusher and warmer sound with a wider variety of tonal capabilities.

The saxophone quartet consists of soprano, alto, tenor, and baritone saxophones with an occasional variance for special effects. The English saxophonist/reviewer Paul Harvey remarked that "The saxophone quartet is capable of playing quietly enough so as not to ruffle the wings of a butterfly but strong enough to overshadow a brass band."

I was honored to be invited to join the New York Saxophone Quartet in 1967. The players were all regarded as New York's top studio musicians and jazz artists. I was thrilled to join the group, especially since it was my first exposure to being a part of such an elite ensemble.

One of our concert tours was to Bordeaux, France in 1974. The purpose primarily was to be part of the World Saxophone Congress hosted by the French saxophone virtuoso Jean-Marie Londeix. During that tour, we played concerts in Bordeaux and at Pays in the Basque area of South France.

Our trip to Bordeaux via Paris from Kennedy Airport got off to a shaky start. We departed about eight hours late thanks to the problems that arose from booking affordable group travel arrangements without a travel agent. In addition, we arrived at Paris Orly Airport when our original destination was supposed to have been at Charles De Gaulle airport. This negatively impacted our schedule by another couple of hours and the extra day meant to acclimate to the jet lag was now thrown into a tizzy. Our group of ten consisted of Ray Beckenstein, his wife Ruth, daughter Cara; Wally Kane, his wife Mary, their two children Elissa and David; Dave Tofani; my ex-wife Charlotte and me.

When finally deplaning at Orly airport our next problem was to get our party of ten across the traffic maze of Paris to the Gare du Nord railway station. Our cab drivers were very cooperative in honoring our request to make haste by going through red lights, driving over sidewalks, and breaking every speed limit in France. Needless to say, it was a bit of a harrowing experience that added to our overall anxiety.

Unloading our luggage, finding the train, and getting our disheveled group over the next hurdle was made further nerve-racking by a fast-talking French redcap handling our bags and advising us to "Allez, allez *hurry up* the next train departs in 15 minutes."

Saxophone Troubadour

I said, "How can we make a train in 15 minutes when it will take us 20 minutes to unload our luggage and get to the other end of the station."

"No, no," the red cap insisted, "We can make it, allez, allez."

We arrived at the departing platform just as the train's conductor was announcing, "All aboard." Knowing at that moment that we could not possibly get on the train in time, we should have thrown in the towel and waited two hours for the next train. Before we could make any decision, the redcap was hurling our luggage onto the last car. When I realized our minds were made up for us, I scurried aboard to assist with our bags that were being thrown carelessly in every direction.

The next thing I knew, the train started moving as Mary Kane was attempting to hand her toddler son up to Wally. At this point, I tore over to the conductor and screamed "Stop the train!"

"No Monsieur" he retorted, "We cannot stop ze train"

In a fit of rage, I pushed him aside and went for the emergency cord. Fortunately, he was a small man whom I had no problem physically moving. As soon as I pulled the cord, an ear-splitting screech was heard and the train came to a lurching, bumpy stop. Just like in the movies.

Our party of ten was exhaustively spent, soaked in perspiration, surrounded by our luggage that was spread out on the aisle of the last car, as we tried to calm our nerves. After several minutes we were approached by two exquisitely uniformed Gendarmes, both of them sporting the trademark French pencil-thin mustaches and wearing their traditional képis (flat-topped circular police hats).

Ray Beckenstein, Dave Tofani, and I were then escorted back to the policemen's private compartment. We received a politely stern admonishment, informing us that the fine for stopping a train was $245.00. We were ready to start the 1974 version of a *real* French/American war, but alas, we paid the fine and went back to our seats quite ticked off.

As so many problems are solved with food in France, their unbelievable cuisine will always come to the rescue. We ended up our travel on the club car of the Bordeaux train from hell with one of the best meals we had during our entire stay in France. This softened our feelings somewhat after the disastrous episode we had just endured.

I had played with the New York Saxophone Quartet for the better part of ten years before leaving them to become saxophone professor at the University of Texas at Austin. There were several tours and concerts which were a wonderful part of my musical life.

After moving to Austin, Texas in 1977 it wasn't long before my thirst for saxophone repertoire resulted in the formation of the Austin Quartet. I have fond memories of the good music we produced if only briefly from 1977 to 1980 in central Texas.

Upon returning to the New York area in 1981 my saxophone madness took over once again and I organized the American Saxophone Quartet. The fabulous talent of this group resulted in a wide variety of repertoire development. Of significance was the making of the CD recording *Gandy Dancer* that was praised worldwide. Prominent American composers Seymour Barab, Calvin Hampton, Bob Mintzer, and Bernard Hoffer wrote works specifically for the group.

In August 1985 the previously mentioned, unexpected death of George Marge shocked us and led to the dissolution of the ensemble. I had the feeling that my saxophone quartet days were over. It was depressing not only that the group no longer existed, but my best friend's death was a profound downer.

After several years without any sax quartet activity of any consequence, I decided once again that my musical life was not complete without serious quartet involvement. The next installment of the American Saxophone Quartet was formed circa 1990 when I asked David Carroll, the New York Philharmonic's associate principal bassoonist if he might be interested in playing tenor saxophone in a quartet. Having a musician such as him was a fabulous asset and one that was the start of the next exciting installment of the ASQ.

David Demsey joined in 1993 and at that point, the group was sounding good and coming together nicely. We were delighted to have the fabulous baritone saxophonist Lino Gomez join us. This ensemble turned out to be the most dedicated and satisfying, as we rehearsed regularly, performed often, had compositions written especially for us, and were fulfilled through several outstanding events.

Concert engagements were many including Carnegie Recital Hall, Merkin Concert Hall in New York City, Teatro Opera in Buenos Aires, and several appearances with the New York Philharmonic. Two CDs entitled *The Commission Project* and *Spanning the River* gained international prominence with *The Commission Project* garnering a Grammy Nomination in 2002. This project combined us with clarinet virtuosi Larry Combs, Paquito D'Rivera, and Ron Odrich.

An outstanding achievement of the ASQ was the commissioning and premiering of Bob Mintzer's *Rhythm of the Americas* for Saxophone Quartet and Orchestra. It was presented at The Kennedy Center in Washington DC on January 24, 25, and 26, 2002 with the National Symphony and Leonard Slatkin conducting. Along with several rave reviews, the composition has received many performances and recordings worldwide. The musical accomplishments, as well as the camaraderie of this ensemble, will always be near to my heart, not only in the personal fulfillment it provided but for its legacy of excellence.

Whatever soul I have comes through in the saxophone and I am grateful every day that it has thoroughly enhanced my life.

ADDENDA: Albert Regni SAX QUARTET HISTORY
Personnel of various saxophone quartets during my tenure

<u>New York Saxophone Quartet</u> (1967 – 1977)
Ray Beckenstein, Soprano Saxophone
Al Regni, Alto Saxophone
Al Epstein, Tenor Saxophone
Frank Perowsky, Tenor Saxophone (1968 – 1969)
Dave Tofani, Tenor Saxophone (1969 – 1977)
Danny Bank, Baritone Saxophone (1967 – 1969)
Wally Kane, Baritone Saxophone (1969 – 1977)

<u>Austin Saxophone Quartet</u> (1977 – 1980)
Al Regni, Soprano Saxophone
Douglas Skinner, Alto Saxophone
Paul Ostermeyer, Tenor Saxophone (1977 – 1979)
Donald Goldstone, Tenor Saxophone (1979 – 1980)
Craig Hearn, Baritone Saxophone (1977 – 1978)
James Warth, Baritone Saxophone (1977 – 1979)

<u>American Saxophone Quartet I</u> (1981 – 1985)
Al Regni, Soprano Saxophone
Jack Kripl, Alto Saxophone
Bob Mintzer, Tenor Saxophone
George Marge, Baritone Saxophone

<u>American Saxophone Quartet II</u> (1990 – 2004)
Al Regni, Soprano Saxophone
David Demsey, Alto Saxophone
David Carroll, Tenor Saxophone
John Winder, Baritone Saxophone
Lino Gomez, Baritone Saxophone

Musings on a Musical Journey

<u>American Saxophone Quartet III</u> (2005 – 2015 Richmond Virginia)
Al Regni, Soprano Saxophone
John Wynn, Alto Saxophone
Gregory Wrenn, Alto Saxophone
George Gailes, Tenor Saxophone
Myrick Crampton, Tenor Saxophone
Jim Nesbit, Baritone Saxophone
Suzette Fisher, Baritone Saxophone

Saxophone Troubadour

Chapter 11
Partial Retirement from NY Music Scene

From my earliest days of performing in New York there were never thoughts or realizations of retiring from being an active musician. I always envisioned the thought of dying with my boots on. How great it would be to play the most gorgeous solo after a long fulfilling career and quickly pass away holding the instrument. But alas, I managed to survive to a ripe old age fairly well unscathed mentally or physically, with many mostly pleasant memories, still yearning for that gorgeous performance.

I like to think that I practice every day to make progress but have come to realize that what we gain in artistic maturity is hampered by physical deterioration of the human body.

Being an active performing musician is much the same as being an athlete. Knowing when to call it quits or at least to modify activities is very important, that is unless you are Tom Brady the indestructible quarterback of the Boston Patriots and the Tampa Bay Buccaneers.

The transition to the next phase of our lives was assisted when my wife Rosy was offered an opportunity to become a professor of fashion merchandising at Virginia Commonwealth University in Richmond, VA. It coincided perfectly with our thoughts of changing course and adjusting to the next stage of life's path. Since we both had successful careers in our respected fields it was now time to take the next step. It really did not require a lot of planning since the stars seemed to be lining up in deciding our fate for us.

Rosy had very wisely purchased land in 1987 along with her college friend Pat Anderson (ne Wiseman) in the town of Manakin Sabot, Virginia not far from Richmond. After several visits we both became attached to this beautiful part of our country and decided it would be a good place to consider for a transition to a stress-free lifestyle. As a result, we had our dreamhouse built on four acres of pristine central Virginia countryside.

It also fulfilled a life-long wish for Rosy that she and her college friends Pat and Jimmie Anderson could live next door to each other.

My wife's teaching position was to begin in 2002 which was a little early for me to make an abrupt break from the music scene that I was involved in. Since playing with the New York Philharmonic, The Metropolitan Opera Orchestra and the New York City Ballet were as an extra, I knew the schedule of performances that I would be involved in for the season. It was reasonable to assume that I could commute and discontinue that work gradually.

After two years of juggling work in New York with trying to adjust to a new life in Richmond it became apparent that the Metropolitan Opera and the New York City Ballet work had to be terminated. The New York Philharmonic became harder to separate from since it was my favorite and the schedule was much easier to maneuver. Commuting by automobile was becoming more difficult and the wear and tear on my body was more evident.

It was hard on Rosy as well, to be left alone in a new house for long periods. After nearly ten years of phasing out

Saxophone Troubadour

of New York City it was now time to make a complete break and keep the home fires burning. Fortunately for me my wife was more supportive and patient than I ever deserved, and we managed to survive the crazy twist our life took for our first twelve years in Richmond, Virginia.

It should also be mentioned that shortly after arriving in Richmond I was offered a job at Virginia Commonwealth University as adjunct professor of saxophone. A full-time position was out of the question but following my life-long pattern of not saying no I accepted a part-time assignment. The transition was also further complicated when I took on five students at the University of Maryland. This lasted for three years when I finally woke up and realized that I was becoming a jack-of-nothing. Automobile commuting was taking over my life. The drive from Richmond, Virginia to College Park, Maryland was something of a nightmare with the traffic in that area being among the worst in the country.

Playing in Washington, D.C. was also adding to my driving schedule and in the first three years of moving to Richmond I was averaging fifty thousand miles of driving a year. It was what-goes-around-comes-around-time and I realized it was a replay of fifty years before, when I was constantly on the road doing big band gigs.

The National Symphony of Washington, D.C. was a thrill to join on occasion since it was such a fine orchestra. It was even more of a joy to be sitting and performing on the same stage as my daughter Marissa. Being the principal second violin in the orchestra she not only held a top position but was hailed by her peers for her high degree of virtuosity as well as her warm humanness. It is difficult to describe the feeling of making music with my daughter especially with that great orchestra. Commuting for one

Musings on a Musical Journey

hour and a half as opposed to the seven hours drive to New York City was also a perc.

Also highlighting my times of playing with the National Symphony was having the opportunity to appear as saxophone soloist. Standing in front of the orchestra while playing the saxophone solo, *A Place in the Sun* by film composer Franz Waxman, conducted by John Williams was another thrill beyond description.

On rare occasions I would travel to the New York area to do recording work with one of my all-time favorite musicians, Angelo DiPippo. Angelo was a first call accordion wizard as well as a composer/arranger and it was always most satisfying and fun to work with him. His sense of humor coupled with his creative skills were a delight.

Since he did most of his recording work in a studio at Glen Cove, Long Island the drive from Richmond was considerably longer than to New York City. This required physical stamina that became more difficult to manage as time passed. Having worked for Angelo for over thirty years transitioning from this phase was among the hardest. He was a good friend as well as a musician that I looked up to.

As the change from life in New York took place, more activities were occurring in the Richmond and Washington, D.C. areas. Playing in the pit for Broadway shows in both towns was fun as the stints were no more than two weeks at a time. This was a pleasant experience after having spent ten years in the pit of *Cats* on Broadway. Eight shows a week for ten years could be a bit of a drain. There were a number of engagements over the years with the Richmond Symphony, an excellent ensemble. Performing at their wonderful Dominion Energy Arts Center with its fine acoustics was a treat.

I have thoroughly enjoyed playing at our church, The Second Baptist Church of Richmond. The choir in residence

Saxophone Troubadour

is very professional and was most ably directed by Bill Miller during the first 17 years of our residence. Bill's retirement in 2019 brought us a fine replacement in Taylor Vancil. The congregation is very culturally adept and wonderfully appreciative of our performances. The beautiful ambience of the church and the fine acoustics have made it a most satisfying performance venue.

A favorite haunt of Rosy and mine is *Cafféspresso* in the west end of Richmond. This is a wonderful Italian coffee house owned by the handsome transplant from Ferrara, Italy Claudio Ragazzi. I think of this café as a treasure of our town and feel as though I am in the middle of Florence, Italy every time I walk through its doors. It is also a place where I have been able to do concerts with a trio and to have celebration parties. Claudio often removes all of the tables and transforms the room into a fabulous mini recital hall. Even though it only seats forty people, it is a dream spot for music making and gatherings. The friends and camaraderie we experienced here have been among the favorite moments of our lives.

More leisure time has opened up new activities such as traveling and going to sports events in Blacksburg, Virginia with our friends and neighbors Jimmie and Pat. I have also joined the Goochland County chapter of the Rotary Club with the dubious distinction to be the oldest person to have ever joined that club as a new member. Who says we're not having fun?

When I first announced to my daughter, Marissa that we were thinking of moving to Richmond, Virginia back in the year 2001, she jokingly remarked, "You won't last down there for more than two weeks."

Truthfully, I had my doubts as well since I had become a hardened New Yorker over the previous fifty years. On the other hand, taking chances and dealing with the challenges involved are what makes life interesting. I always believed that change is a good thing.

Now that retirement is in full swing, I spend a good portion of every day devoted to music. It has been an honor to have my full library of saxophone music accepted into William Paterson's University Living Jazz Archives located in Wayne, New Jersey. The archives are curated by my good friend David Demsey.

Richmond has proven to be more than satisfying for Rosy and me. We have found much happiness, culture, friends, a meaningful church life and very importantly, fine food. Spending more time together, especially during the dreadful Covid 19 pandemic, has brought us even closer together. I am happy to say that it was a great move, and we intend to be here for the entire run.

So, music has treated me well and all-in-all life is good.

Conclusion

I am writing this in my 85th year. Feeling pretty good, that is from the chin up. The rag-time pianist Eubie Blake once proclaimed at age 95, "If I knew I was going to live this long, I would have taken better care of myself" bears noting here.

After over 60 years of being a professional musician, I have much to be grateful for. Being part of such a noble profession has been an honor. There certainly have been some down moments, but for the most part, it has been a very smooth ride and I feel like I earned my stripes.

Growing up during the 1940s and experiencing the culture of the mid 20th century has left an indelible mark. My earliest influences came mainly through jazz music and *The Great American Songbook*. The music of George Gershwin, Irving Berlin, Cole Porter as well as Charlie Parker, Paul Desmond, and Miles Davis are among the motivators that forged my path and continue to do so. It wasn't until my college days that I delved into classical music and learned of the cultural depths of Bach, Mozart, Beethoven, and the many scores of composers who brought so much joy to my life.

The first music that really caught my attention and lit the flame was during the 1940s when hearing the likes of Charlie Parker, Dizzy Gillespie, and Miles Davis and the music of the *Be-Bop* period. Tunes such as *Billy's Bounce, Donna Lee,* and *Four* were at the top of my list.

The excitement at first hearing this music on LP and 45 records was only exceeded by the elation of making an attempt at playing them. This for me laid the basic concepts of practice and the persistence it took to perform satisfactorily. The music also set a foundation for the disciplines that helped in my music development as well as for the fundamentals of life.

There were a number of tunes that caught my fancy. Many of them were written by Charlie Parker, Miles Davis, Tadd Dameron, and Dizzy Gillespie. This was the modern music of my formative years and what I most related to. The challenges that learning to play much of this music on saxophone created an early incentive builder. The tune *Four* was composed in 1954, which was my first year in college.

Four remains one that I continue to love playing because of its chord changes that are wonderful for improvisation. Hearing Stan Getz's 1955 recording still is amazing and brings me goosebumps. This jazz standard by Miles Davis plus the clever lyrics by Eddie Jefferson are uncomplicated, but for me capture the basic essence of jazz. I cite this as an example of a mantra that has propelled my love of music and life.

Of the wonderful things that you get out of life,
there are four
And they may not be many,
but nobody needs any more
Of the many facts making the list of life
Truth takes the lead
And to relax knowing the gist of life
It's truth you need
Then the second is honor and

Saxophone Troubadour

happiness makes number three
When you put them together you know
what the last one must be
Baby so truth, honor, and happiness
And one thing more,
Meaning only wonderful, wonderful love
That will make it four

Learning some of the basics of jazz improvisation early on-set rules of basic life disciplines that distinctly carry over into good life practices. Finding the right note that "fits" at any given moment I believe is a quest for truth. Sometimes it can be an accidental surprise or at other times a dismal failure but in either case, with the proper intent, it is a realization of an honest pursuit.

Having had a rather late start in being introduced to classical music was a bit of a shock when I first entered college. During my first week at the conservatory, a preliminary questionnaire asked me to name my three favorite classical composers. It was embarrassing to think, here I was beginning professional music training and only able to name two, Bach and Beethoven. For the third, I chose Stan Kenton whose Neophonic Jazz Band was the closest I came to classical indoctrination.

This was the first realization that while I thought of myself as having a good background, I was decidedly a greenhorn with so much to learn. Humbling to say the least. Getting acclimated to this new phase in my life took some major attitude readjustment. When beginning to realize what went into the creations of Bach, Mozart, Verdi, Shostakovich, and so many others, the wondrous powers of music overtook my life.

When recollecting about who and what my main motivators were, I have many individuals to thank. Some of them because of the encouragement that they generously gave and a few who through their honest negative opinions of my abilities made me mad enough to prove them wrong. I spent a fair amount of time in psychotherapy dealing with the anger and obsessions that I carried for several years as a result. I would sometimes wonder if what drove me was a love of music or a reason to show my doubters that I could cut the mustard.

As many of us do, the need to satisfy our parents is a main motivator in our actions. My father was a product of early practices of using intimidation, put-downs, and fear in parenting. He could be very encouraging at times but would often turn to belittlement as a way of thinking he was helping. This could be very frustrating especially when he would use what he thought was humor in deprecating our mother. It could be hard to love him at times but as I age the need to forgive has taken over and I have come to realize that he did the best he could. In the final analysis, I feel that he loved us. In retrospect that has become one of my life's satisfactions.

It is gratifying to realize that I do really love music. It brings a chuckle to think that after all of these years and the endless lonely hours in the practice room that it took me the better part of eighty-five years to figure out that fact of my life.

Now that I no longer need to prepare for tomorrow's gig, I still feel the need to practice and get the sounds right. I feel the need to send a beautiful note to eternity soaring like a rocket with an endless ray of beauty. I know I'm a dreamer but do believe that someone or some being will hear it and be happy. To me, that is the beauty of making music.

Speaking of beauty, I couldn't conclude this without being grateful for my entire amazing family. I don't know what I did to get to this point, but things have been right on. Spending more time with Rosy has been a joy, especially during the dreadful pandemic years of 2020 and 2021. Life has been and is good.

Musings on a Musical Journey

Acknowledgements

I have many people to thank along the way, some of whose names I can't even recall. The journey has taken me through many twists and turns and has been a constant learning experience. From teachers to colleagues to friends to people at a variety of concerts, recording sessions, and gigs, some I never actually met but with whom I made music. There was so much to be grateful for in just having the opportunity to be part of a unified effort with so many talented and dedicated human beings. I would be amiss if I didn't mention at least a few of the distinguished artists that inspired and brought such joy and beauty to my life.

The virtuosity of my daughter Marissa Elizabeth Regni has been my primary joy as I watched her grow into the first-class violinist that she has become over the years. Her brilliance has never ceased to amaze me along with the constant source of love and inspiration. Artists such as Al Gallodoro and Jimmy Abato, saxophonists extraordinaire, were huge influences from the age of 12 when I wore out vinyl recordings in an attempt to match their artistry. They were certainly the first igniters of the spark. My first saxophone teacher, Gino Calistri of Binghamton New York, gave my mind's ear an ever-present source of a warm saxophone sound. My high school music teachers Donal

Saxophone Troubadour

O'Buckley and Kenneth Myers gave me excellent direction to becoming a musician.

During my college years, I was fortunate to have had a clarinet professor William Osseck who not only taught me symphonic clarinet repertoire but provided know-how in orchestral saxophone playing techniques that proved useful throughout my career. Fellow students at the Eastman School of Music were influential in their abilities and musical concepts. Sydney Hodkinson and John Veith were student colleagues who laid an invaluable foundation.

My best and life-long friend George Marge was a huge inspiration and also a fellow student at the Eastman School. He was not only a colleague but also a mentor, advisor, confidant, and all-around mensch. He was a first-class musician and human being who accomplished so much in a life that ended much too soon at the age of 53.

Having been the principal saxophonist with the New York Philharmonic for the better part of 50 years was a blessing beyond description. To have sat alongside musicians of such high caliber was a thrill of a lifetime not to mention scary. Two of the world's greatest flutists, Julius Baker and Paige Brook were not only an inspiration to hear but ever-present in giving invaluable professional and artistic advice.

The great clarinet wizard Stanley Drucker was an instrumentalist of supreme skill. His tenure in the orchestra surpassed 60 years while he retained a youthful spirit throughout. Joseph Alessi, trombonist, whose world-class abilities were dazzling on every note that he played. Phil Smith, the epitome of an all-around trumpet artist with a capital A. The incomparable concertmasters John Corigliano, Sr. and Glenn Dicterow whose abilities were as top-notch as the humble humanity that they possessed.

Musings on a Musical Journey

These were but a few of the wonderful New York Philharmonic artists that I am so thankful to have associated with.

Bob Mintzer, the incredible jazz saxophonist, has constantly amazed me with the depth of his skills as an instrumentalist, conductor, composer, and arranger. I deeply treasure his friendship. His strengths in a host of musical genres are only matched by his caring and kindness.

Last but certainly the greatest thanks go to my incredible wife Rosalie Jackson Regni, better known as Rosy. She has been a force that I can't begin to describe in the inspiration and continued support she has given throughout these past 32 years. This memoir would not have been possible without her invaluable encouragement.

–March 2022, Manakin Sabot, Virginia

Saxophone Troubadour

Al Regni Career Resumé

EDUCATION
BACHELOR OF MUSIC *Eastman School of Music, 1958*
Rochester, N.Y., Clarinet, Public School Music
PERFORMER'S CERTIFICATE Eastman 1958
Rochester, N.Y., Clarinet
MASTER OF MUSIC Manhattan School of Music, 1961
New York City, N.Y., Clarinet
GRADUATE STUDIES American University, 1959-60
Washington D.C.
ACADEMIC AWARD
2019 Distinguished Alumni Award - Eastman School of Music

INSTRUMENTAL TEACHERS

Saxophone	Clarinet
Joseph Allard	Leon Russianoff
William Osseck	Herbert Blayman
Gino Calistri	William Osseck
Joe Napolean	
Flute	Vocal Tone Production
Harold Bennett	Elsa Seyfert
Samuel Baron	
Francis Blaisdell	
Paige Brook	

FRATERNAL AFFILIATIONS
Sinfonia (Phi Mu Alpha)- Eastman School of Music
Pi Kappa Lambda (Honor Society) University of Texas

MILITARY SERVICE
The U.S. Army Band, Washington, D.C., 1958-1961 (Pershing's Own)

TEACHING
University of Texas at Austin (Austin, Texas) - 1977-80,
Tenured Associate Professor of Saxophone

Musings on a Musical Journey

The College of New Jersey (Trenton, N.J.) 1986–2000,
Professor of Saxophone
Eastman School of Music (Rochester, N.Y.) 1988 & 2001
Visiting Professor of Saxophone
State University of New York (Purchase) 1972–1977,
Affiliate Artist (Saxophone and Clarinet)
New York University (New York City, 1992-1994)
Kings College (Armonk, N.Y.) 1965–1969,
Adjunct Professor of Saxophone
Kingsborough College (New York City, N.Y.) 1970–77,
Adjunct Professor of Saxophone
Bard College (Annandale-on-Hudson, N.Y.) 1975–77,
Adjunct Professor of Saxophone and Clarinet
Lehman College (New York City, N.Y.) 1980–1993
Adjunct Professor of Saxophone
University of Maryland (College Park, MD.) 2014–2018
Adjunct Professor of Saxophone
Virginia Commonwealth University (Richmond, Va.) 2002–2018
Adjunct Professor of Saxophone

PROFESSIONAL EXPERIENCE

ORCHESTRAL AND CHAMBER MUSIC
New York Philharmonic (Saxophone), 1963-2013 (Principal Saxophonist)
Metropolitan Opera Orchestra (Saxophone/Bass Clarinet 1988-2004[Principal Sax]
New York City Ballet (Saxophone), 1968-2010 [Principal Saxophonist]
New York City Opera Orchestra (clarinet -Eb clarinet)
American Composer's Orchestra (Saxophone Soloist)
American Symphony Orchestra (Bass Clarinet-Saxophone
American Saxophone Quartet (S Saxophone 1981 - 2017
New York Saxophone Quartet (Alto Sax),1968—1977
World Saxophone Congress Soloist, Toronto, Canada, (Performer), 1972
Leningrad Philharmonic (Sax), U.S. Tour, 1973
Philadelphia Symphony Orchestra

Saxophone Troubadour

Baltimore Symphony Orchestra
National Symphony Orchestra (Washington, D.C.
(Saxophone Soloist)
St. Petersburg Philharmonic (Russia) (Saxophonist 1996 & 2000 Carnegie Hall)
Israel Philharmonic, US, Israel and European Tours, 1986 and 1988
Rotterdam Philharmonic (Holland), U.S. Tour, 1987
Steven Reich Ensemble <u>Clarinet and Flute Soloist</u> (Spain), 1987
World Saxophone Congress, Bordeaux, France, 1974
Los Angeles Philharmonic
Chamber Music Society of Lincoln Center
Orpheus Ensemble
The Austin Saxophone Quartet
New York Philharmonic Prospective Encounters
(Chamber Music Series with Pierre Boulez)
Marlboro Music Festival, (Participant -1972) Clarinet, Bass Clarinet & Saxophone
Aspen Music Festival
Vail, Colorado Summer Festival
Teton Music Festival, (With New York Philharmonic)
Cabrillo (California) Music Festival (soloist)
Edinborough Music Festival (Scotland)
Odessa (Russia) Philharmonic Soloist
Concordia Orchestra (New York)
Lake Placid Symphonette (Saxophone Soloist) St. Lukas Chamber Orchestra and Ensemble
Rochester Philharmonic
Eastman-Rochester Orchestra (Clarinet Soloist)
Royal Ballet Orchestra
Joffrey Ballet Orchestra
Stuttgart Ballet Orchestra
Soho Chamber Ensemble, (Saxophone Soloist)
Gramercy Arts Ensemble
Bronx Arts Ensemble
Group for Contemporary Music (Soloist and Performer)
Performer's Committee for Contemporary Music, (Columbia University)
Brooklyn Philharmonic
Westchester Symphony

Musings on a Musical Journey

Radio City Music Hall Orchestra
Speculum Musicae
Contemporary Chamber Ensemble, (A. Weisberg)
The Berlin Opera Ballet Orchestra
Caecilian Society, (Saxophone Soloist)
White Mountains Music Festival (New Hampshire) (Saxophone Soloist)
St. Paul Chamber Orchestra (Saxophone Soloist)
Teton Music Festival, (With New York Philharmonic)
American Ballet Theatre Orchestra
Rob Fisher Coffee Club Orchestra, Garrison Keillor Radio Show (PBS 6 Seasons)

New York Philharmonic Tours
1968 - U.S. Southern and Mid-West
1970 - Japan
1970 - Southern U.S.
1975 - Europe
1976 - Europe
1976 - Mid-West U.S
1978 - South American -Dominican Republic
1983 - South American
1984 - Europe
1986 - South America
1988 - Russia
1989 - Europe and United States
1991 - South America and U.S.
1992 - South America
1993 - Europe
1995 - European Festivals
1996 - Europe
1997 - South America
1998 - Asia
1999 - North America
2000 - Spain
2000 - China, Philippines, Singapore, Japan

2003 - Sardinia
2004 - South Korea & Japan
2006 - Europe
2008 - North Korea/ China
2010 – England

Metropolitan Opera Orchestra Tours
1992 - Spain
1993 - Japan
1995 - North America
2000 - Spain, Portugal, Canary Islands
2001 - Europe
2002 - Europe

Washington DC National Symphony Tours
2005 West Coast U.S.
2005 -2015 Orchestra Residencies in Arkansas and South Carolina

Liza Minnelli U.S. and Far East Tour (Japan, Australia Philippines, Hawaii, China) <u>1981</u>

RECORDINGS
NEW YORK PHILHARMONIC
SAXOPHONE (CLARINET/ BASS CLARINET)

Ravel	Bolero	Pierre Boulez	Columbia
Ravel	Bolero	Kurt Mazur	Teldac
Berg	Lulu Suite	Boulez	Columbia
Berg	Lulu Suite	Thomas Schippers	Columbia
Berg	Lulu Suite	Mazur	Teldac
Bartok	Wooden Prince	Boulez	DG
Shostakovich	Golden Age	Bernstein	Columbia
Moussorgsky-Ravel Pictures at An Exhibition			
		Thomas	Columbia
Prokofieff	Lt. Kije	Bernstein	Columbia
Shostakovitch	Golden Age	Bernstein	Columbia

Musings on a Musical Journey

Foss	Phorion	Bernstein	Columbia
Berio	Symphonia	Bernstein	Columbia
Gershwin	American in Paris	Tilson-Thomas	Columbia
Stravinsky (Bass Cl.)	Rite of Spring	Mehta	Columbia
Bartok	Village Scenes	Boulez	Columbia
Kodaly	Harry Janos Suite	Mazur	Teldac

Moussorgsky -Ravel Pictures at An Exhibition
                    Sinnopoli   D G

Prokofief	Romeo & Juliet	Mazur	Teldac
Gershwin (Fazil Say)		Mazur	Teldec

I got Rhythm Variations, Rhapsody in Blue

RECORDINGS WITH THE METROPOLITAN OPERA ORCHESTRA

Moussorgsky/Ravel Pictures at An Exhibition		Levine	DG
Berg	Lulu Suite	Levine	DG
Berg	Wozzeck	Levine	DG
Stravinsky	Rite of Spring	Levine (Bass Clarinet)	DG
Berg	3 Pieces Op. 6	Levine (clarinet)	DG

OTHER CLASSICAL RECORDINGS

Bernstein. West Side Story (Principal Clarinet)		Bernstein	Dutch Gram.
Bernstein MASS		Bernstein	Columbia
Gershwin	Rhapsody in Blue (Grammy winner)	Tilson-Thomas	Columbia
Perle	Serenade #3	Schwarz	Nonesuch
Milhaud	Creation Du Monde	Weisberg	Nonesuch
Weill	Stratas sings Weill	Schwarz	Nonesuch
Weill	Three-Penny Operas	Weisberg	Nonesuch
Weill	Three-Penny Opera	Rudel	Music Masters
Walton	Facade	Arthur Fiedler /Tony Randall	Columbia
Babitt	All Set.	Weisberg	Nonesuch
Weisgall	The Stronger	Weissgall	CRI
T.J. Anderson	Var on a Theme by M.B. Tolsen	Weisberg	Nonesuch
Harbison	Bermuda Triangle	Harbison	CRI
J.K. Randall	Improvisation	Gilbert	CRI
Gershwin	Concerto in F	Schuller/St Lukes	ProArte

Saxophone Troubadour

Gershwin Let 'em Eat Cake Michael Tilson-Thomas   CBS
& Of Thee I Sing   St. Luke's   CBS
John Adams Nixon in China Edo De Waart   Elektra
St Lukes   Deutche Grammaphone
Gershwin Songs with Kiri Tikanawa   McGlenn   EMI
Gershwin Overtures   McGlenn   EMI
Sondheim Collection   Various Book of the Month
Sondheim Songs of New York Gemignani   Book of the Month
Bernstein Jubilee Games
Bernstein Angel (with Israel Phil)
Grofe' Grand Canyon Suite   S. Richmond ~Harmonie Ensemble
Grofe' Mississippi Suite   S. Richmond ~Harmonie Ensemble
Gershwin I Got Rhythm Variations / Rhapsody in Blue – Harmonie Ensemble

JAZZ-POP PERFORMANCES/RECORDINGS: (Partial List)

Garrison Keilor	Angelo Di Pippo	David Lynch
Bob Mintzer	Rob Fisher	Angelo Badalamenti
Pat Martino	Charles Mingus	Don Sebesky
Roberta Flack	Debbie Reynolds	Joe Jackson
Liza Minelli	George Benson	Melba Moore
Julie Andrews	Modern Jazz Qt.	Placido Domingo
Stephen Sondheim	Peter Duchin	Livingston Taylor
Betty Carter	Jewel	Kristen Chenowith
Robert Goulet	Itzhak Perlman	Charles Mingus
Marianne Faithful	James Galway	Leonard Bernstein
Nancy Wilson	Judy Collins	David Bowie
Paquito D'Rivera	David Raksin	Johnny Green
Sid Ramin	John Williams	Marvin Hamlisch
Burt Bacharach	Tony Bennett	Jonathan Tunick

Musings on a Musical Journey

TELEVISION
West – Side Story / Bernstein, Carraras TV Documentary Principal Clarinet)
Performances on documentary and dramatic TV films for CBS, PBS, ABC, NBC, WNET, METROMEDIA, including "The Adams Chronicles," "Forbidden City," "Camera Three," "Sunday Morning," "Live From Lincoln Center" for PBS; Numerous Documentaries; TV Soap Operas "All My Children," "The Guiding Light," "General Hospital," etc. "Twin Peaks" (GOLD RECORD) (Solo Saxophone, Clarinet, and Bass Clarinet Soloist and Grammy); NBC & ABC Sports Themes, McNeil-Lehar News Hour PBS

CARTOONS
Disney; Mighty Mouse; Thunder Cats; Silver Hawks, Karate Kats, The New Adventures of Mighty Mouse

MOVIES
*Hester Street   Cape Fear
The Happy Hooker
House Sitters
Blue Velvet
Mad Dog and Glory
Fire Walk With Me
Twin Peaks
Ishtar
Get on the Bus
Crooklyn
Beauty and the Beast
Clockers
The Fantasticks
The Last Good Time
Life and Adventures of Santa Claus
My Blue Heaven
Law and Disorder
Power
Raggedy Ann
Shattered
It's Our World Too
In & Out
Femme Fatale
Pocahontas
The Hunchback of Notre Dame
Auto Focus
Double Platinum
Home Alone II
The Manchurian Candidate*

TELEVISION/RADIO COMMERCIALS
Numerous, including: MacDonald's; Timex; Remington; American Express, Visa, American, Eastern, Pan Am, and Delta Airlines; Volkswagen; Discover, Millers Beer, Budweiser Christmas, Tourneau Corner, ExLax, Texaco; Chrysler, Cadillac, Ford, Chevrolet, Merrill-Lynch, Dodge, Chrysler etc.

Saxophone Troubadour

NAME BANDS
Benny Goodman
National Jazz Ensemble (original Band)
Warren Covington/Tommy Dorsey
Larry Elgart - Les Elgart
Richard Maltby
Sammy Kaye
Rob Fisher's Coffee Club Orchestra with American Radio Company

BROADWAY SHOWS [on Broadway, New York City]
Shenandoah (3 years)
Passion
Victor Victoria
Twigs (solo saxophone)
Captains Courageous
On the Town
Company
Peter Pan
Funny Girl (3 years)
Bajour
Pajama Gam
El Bravo
Brigadoon (Brdway revival)
The Ambassadors
Louisiana Purchase
Chicago
The Petrified Prince
West Side Story (TV Doc.)
Bernstein's Mass
Coco
Big
Seesaw
Out of this World
Mata Hari
Stop the World
Cats (10 years)
Seven Brides for 7 Brothers
Angel
Grand Night for Singing
The Goodbye Girl
Over Here
Jesus Crist, Superstar
Fig Leaves are Falling
The Happy Time

PERFORMANCES, RECORDINGS WITH THE FOLLOWING CONDUCTORS:
Leonard Bernstein
Pierre Boulez
Eric Leinsdorf
Zubin Mehta
Leopold Stokowski
Pablo Casals
William Walton
Karl Anceral
Andre Kostelanetz
Lucas Foss
Jose Iturbi
Karl Bohm
Seiji Ozawa
Andrew Davis
Lorin Maazel
David Gilbert
Danny Kaye
John Adams
James Conlon
Ricardo Muti
Sir Colin Davis
Robert Spano
Arthur Weisberg
Charles Dutoit
Mariss Jensins
Gerard Schwarz
Danny Kaye

Musings on a Musical Journey

Arthur Fiedler	Luciano Berio	Jacob Druckman
Morton Gould	Bruno Maderna	Hans Werner Henze
Andre Previn	James Levine	Yuri Temirkov
Maxim Shostakovich	Thomas Schippers	
Kazuroshi Akiyama	Kurt Mazur	William Steinberg
Bernard Haitink	Rafael Kubelik	
Gennadi Nicolas Rozhdestvensky		David Robertson
Leonard Slatkin	Valerie Gregarov	
David Robertson	John Williams	Gianandrea Noseda

SOLO SAXOPHONE RECORDINGS

Albert Regni **Extended Saxophone**	CRI
Albert Regni **Three Dark Paintings**	Open Loop
Albert Regni **El Amor**	Sons of Sound
Al Regni **Revisiting the Silver Screen**	Titanic
Al Regni **Revisiting the Great White Way**	Titanic
American Saxophone Quartet	
Gandy Dancer	Sons of Sound
Spanning The River	Sons of Sound
The Commission Project	Sons of Sound

SAXOPHONE SOLOIST WITH:

The New York Philharmonic - (John Williams)
The National Symphony – (John Williams and Leonard Slatkin)
Contemporary Chamber Ensemble - (Arthur Weisberg)
The University of Texas Wind Ensemble - (Tom Lee)
American Composer's Orchestra - (David Gilbert and Dennis Russell Davies)
Westlake High School Band - (Lee Boyd Montgomery)
Wayne Chamber Orchestra - (Murray Colosimo)
The Little Orchestra Society - (Dino Anagnost)
NY Chamber Soloists
Virginia Commonwealth University Wind ensemble (Terry Austin)
Lake Placid Symphonette (David Gilbert)
The College of New Jersey Wind Ensemble

CONTEST ADJUDICATOR

Texas State Solo and Ensemble - 1978
Texas State Solo and Ensemble - 1979
New York Young Concert Artist Guild Competition Judge
Texas All-State - 1979
Chamber Music America Magazine Panelist/Judge 2000-2001

MASTER CLASS/CLINICS

University of Texas, Austin, Texas
Cabrillo Music Festival, California
Aspen Music Festival, Colorado
White Mountain Music Festival, N.H.
Sam Houston State University, Huntsville, Texas
New York State Teachers' Convention (1976)
Hewlett High School, Hewlett, Long Island
Eastman School of Music, Rochester, N.Y.
Peabody Conservatory, Baltimore, Md.
High School of Performing Arts, Baltimore, Md.
Southwest Texas State University
Conservatorium, Sydney, Australia
Hartt College of Music, West Hartford, Conn.
The College of New Jersey
Carnegie Mellon University
Virginia Commonwealth University
Kutztown University, Pennsylvania
Jersey City State College, NJ
University of Maryland, College Park, MD.

Musings on a Musical Journey

SHORT LIST of distinguished students

Ramon Ricker	Sax Prof., Eastman School of Music
David Demsey	Sax Professor, Wm. Paterson College
Lino Gomez	NY Phil, Met Opera, NY City Ballet
Douglas Skinner	Saxophone Prof.,Southwest Texas U.
Donald Harrison	Renowned Jazz Artist
Kenny Garrett	Renowned Jazz Artist
Phil Thompson	North Carolina U. Sax Professor
James Warth	Nova Saxophone Quartet
Rob Lockart	L.A. Movie/TV Studio Musician
Gregory Wilson	Sax Prof., Southwest Texas Univ.
Dan Goble	Sax Prof., Colorado State Univ.U.
Charles Pillow	NY City Broadway, Studio Musician,
Paul Ostermayer	NY City Broadway, Studio Musician
John Winder	NY City Broadway, Studio Musician
Dave Reikenberg	NY City Broadway, Studio Musician,
Mike Chamberland	U.S. Army Jazz Ambassadors
Mike Hashim	International Jazz artist
Jack Murray	Charlotte, NC - East Coast freelancer
Bob Sands	Madrid, Spain, Jazz artist
Brent Stanton	Australian/American Woodwind artist

Special Thanks

I have quite a number of people to thank for guiding me through the ins and outs of what it takes to put words onto a page in a somewhat literate fashion.

Thanks again to my precious wife Rosy whose excellent direction led me through the entire process with an overabundance of love, encouragement, persistence, and God knows, patience.

To Mike Sisti for his guidance and skills into all the important facets of printing, publishing, photo knowhow and long phone advice sessions.

To Ron Odrich, the modern-day renaissance man who, as a world class periodontist, clarinetist, artist, novelist, multi-linguist, and video producer, took the time to diligently editing and making it seem like I knew what I was doing.

To the countless number of wonderful musicians who were such an inspiration for my need to muse on a wonderful journey.

Al Regni
Through the Years

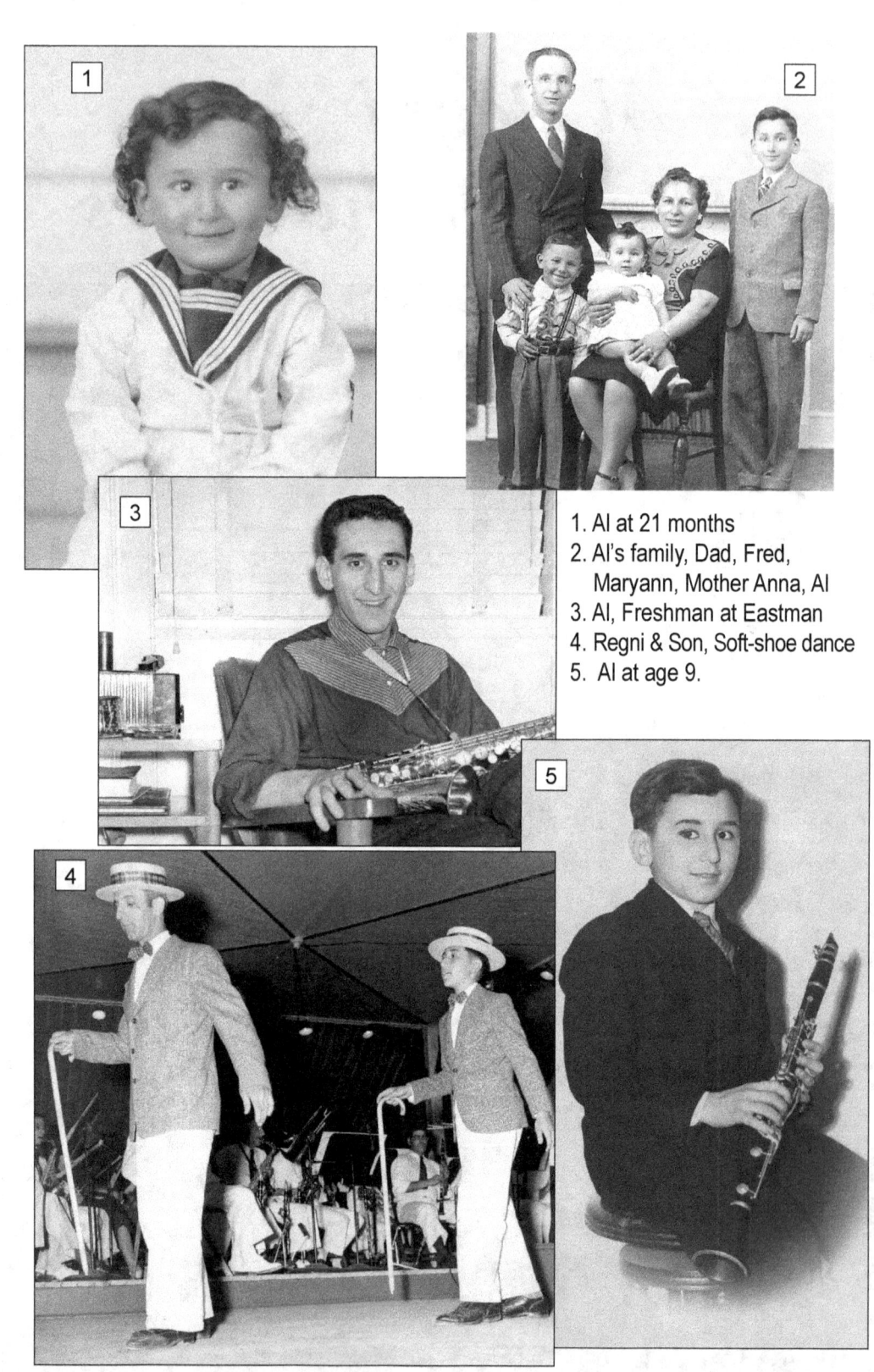

1. Al at 21 months
2. Al's family, Dad, Fred, Maryann, Mother Anna, Al
3. Al, Freshman at Eastman
4. Regni & Son, Soft-shoe dance
5. Al at age 9.

1. Al's dad, Circa 1944
2. NY Sax Quartet 1976, Colorado
3. Al at Eastman Performer's Cert. concert
4. EJ Band, Binghamton NY 1945
5. West Side Story reeds, recording session 1985 at RCA

1. Before NY Carnegie Hall concert 1985
2. Soloing at Rainbow Room, NYC, with Joe Alessi Band
3. Seymour Barab, Bernie Hoffer, Al
4. American Saxophone Quartet, 1983
   Jack Kripl, Bob Mintzer, Al, George Marge

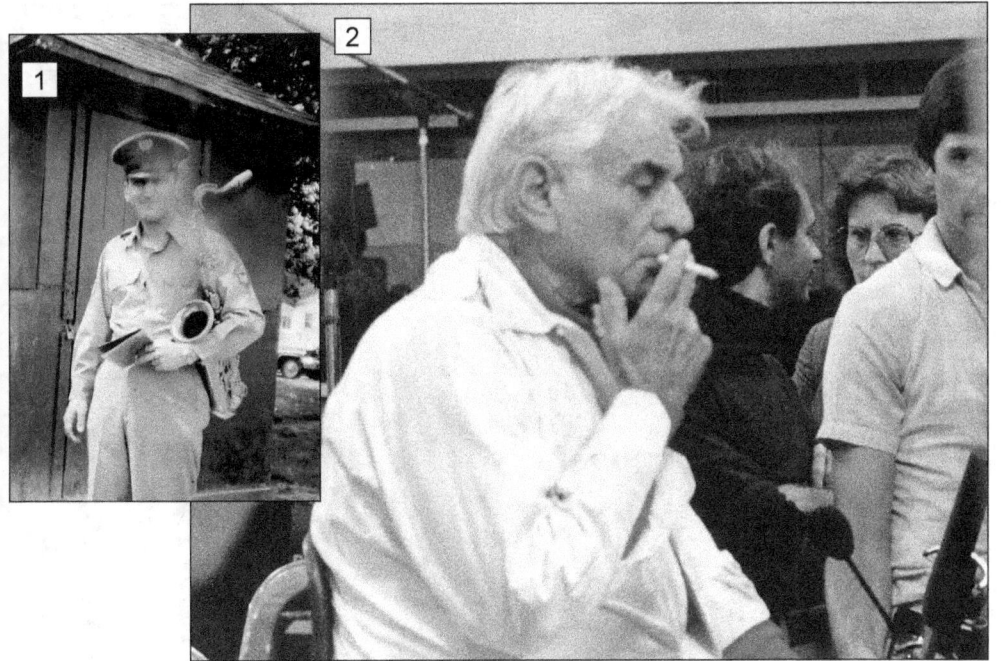

1. Al with US Army Band, 1960
2. Leonard Bernstein West Side Story recording, 1985
3. Al with NY Philharmonic Brass section, Tokyo Yamaha, 1970
4. Al with Stanley Drucker

1. Al and friends at Caffespresso
2. Regni Archives, Wm. Paterson Univ. Dan Willis, Ron Odrich, Dave Dempsey, Al
3. American Sax Quartet
4. Chamber Music: Laurie Hamilton, Dorothy Strahl, Al, Lanny Pakin

1. Distinguished Alumni Award, Eastman College, 2019
2. American Saxophone Quartet Central Park, NYC
3. Al & Rosy (Photo credit: E. Frawley)

1. Marissa (Photo credit: Kevin Lamarque)
2. Granddaughter Sofie, 2021
3. Rosy, Al and Sofie, 2004

www.ingramcontent.com/pod-product-compliance
Lightning Source LLC
Chambersburg PA
CBHW071959070526
44583CB00015B/1253